The Life and Legacy
of
Peter The Great

Famous trotting sire from Kalamazoo

Terry Motycka
Roxy Publishing
Portage, Michigan
2006

Roxy Publishing, Portage, Michigan 49024
Copyright© 2006 by Terry Motycka
Website   http://web.mac.com/terrymotycka

Published 2006
Printed in the United States of America

Fourth printing

Library of Congress Publishers-Cataloging-in-Publication Data

Motycka, Terry. (Therese M.)
The life and legacy of Peter The Great/Terry Motycka
    p. cm. - 21.6x28
Includes bibliographical references, index, and illustrations.
Contents: The story of the life and legacy of famous trotting sire Peter The Great.
Forebears -- Early years -- Racing years -- Breeding years -- Grave and monuments -- Honors and accolades -- Famous progeny -- Epilogue.
    ISBN 10   1-4243-1163-2 (soft cover)
    ISBN 13   978-1-4243-1163-7
1. Harness trotting sire—U. S. biography. 2. Harness racing history—non-fiction literature. 3. Trotting sire lines—non-fiction literature. [1. Harness trotting sire—U. S. biography. 2. Harness racing history. 3. Trotting sire lines.] 1. Title.
798.4—dc22

Acknowledgement:

The author and publisher(s) are grateful to The Harness Racing Museum & Hall of Fame, Goshen, New York, copyright holder of <u>The American Trotter</u> by John Hervey, which acknowledges the author's use of material from that book. Such acknowledgement does not warrant or assume any legal liability or responsibility for the accuracy and/or completeness of any information disclosed.

Covers:

Cover photograph (front) reproduced with permission of the Western Michigan University Archives and Regional History Collections; cover photograph (back) reproduced with permission of the U. S. Trotting Association. See Illustration Credits for identification of images.

Disclaimer:

Every effort has been made to contact copyright holders of any material used/reproduced in this book. Any omissions will be rectified in subsequent printings if sufficient notice is given to the publishers.

Printed on ∞ acid-free paper by Fidlar Doubleday.

~

*This book
is dedicated jointly
to my husband Jim and my eleven-year old grandson Cody*

~ ~ ~

...to Jim, for the Peter The Great adventures we have shared, last spring seeking out the monument to Peter in Kalamazoo, standing together, reading the words inscribed on the bronze plaque; afterwards, knocking at the door of The Oaklands, and being invited in for an impromptu and quite fascinating visit. The adventure continued last summer, when we went to French Lick; while there, we visited the peaceful glade where Peter's other monument stands, imagining the whispers of yesteryear on the wind as we read the words etched on the monument's façade.

~ ~ ~

...and to Cody, who two years ago bought for me for Christmas, out of his own money, a journal I treasure, a spiral-bound book covered in the spotted golds and blacks of faux leopard fur. Cody knew I wanted to write a book, and thought the journal would give me a good start. Cody's unflagging interest has meant more to me that he can possibly know.

~ ~ ~

*...And ultimately, I find that there is yet one more:
this book must also be dedicated to*

Peter The Great

~

Table of Contents

Acknowledgements   ix

Introduction   xi

Overview   1

Part One   The Forebears   3

Part Two   The Early Years   13

Part Three   The Racing Years   25

Part Four   The Breeding Years   45

Part Five   Peter's Grave & Monuments   61

Part Six   Honors & Accolades   73

Part Seven   Peter's Progeny   85

Epilogue   98

Afterword   101

Timeline   105

Chronological List of Races   107

Races in Order of Wins, Seconds & Thirds   108

Stud Career   109

Famous Forebears   110

Pedigree Page   111

Harness Racing Today   112

Notes   114

Sources Consulted   127

Illustration Credits   131

Index   133

Acknowledgements

The author wishes to thank the following people for their help with research on Peter The Great: they have provided written materials, vintage photographs, conversations (both verbal and via email), or help of another kind.

Written Materials, Vintage Photographs, Other Help (Local)
Sharon Carlson, Director of the Western Michigan University Archives and Regional History Collections; Catherine A. Larson of the Kalamazoo Public Library Local History Collections; Rebecca Pierce (Editor), Ann Holcomb (Archivist), and Dave Hager (History/Staff Writer) of the Kalamazoo Gazette; Paula Metzner (Asst. Director of Collections Services) and Tom Dietz, (Curator of Research) of the Kalamazoo Valley Museum; John Urschel, Director of the Kalamazoo Records Management Facility; Rosanna Metoyer of WMU Auxiliary Enterprises/The Oaklands; and Jacob Arndt, former Resident Manager of The Oaklands.

Written Materials, Vintage Photographs, Historical Conversations, Other Help
The late John Hervey, author of *The American Trotter* (used courtesy of The Harness Racing Museum & Hall of Fame, Goshen, New York); the late Ken McCarr, harness racing historian; the late Leon W. Miller and the *Michigan History Magazine*; Dean A. Hoffman and the U. S. Trotting Association; the *Indianapolis Star Magazine; The Horse Review;* Suzanne Stanis of the Historical Landmark Foundation of Indiana; Ronald B. Wiser and Associates Financial Planners of Kalamazoo for providing the website comparing monetary amounts in the 19th century with those of today; Patti Watson and Jim Marshall of the West Baden Springs Dome Hotel/Historic Landmark; Eva-Sharon Kobee, and the French Lick Springs Resort, for permission to use map of the French Lick area; Bob Lane (tour guide at both hotels named above), especially for conversations, and for articles given to him by the sister of Jake Councilman; Roger Stuckman, especially for his stories of French Lick and the article *Tribute To a Master Breeder* written in 1894; Jane and Jim Holmes of the American Legion in Indianapolis, Indiana; Mick and Judy Heenan, owners of Bitter-Sweet Acres Belgians (located in Bloomingdale, Michigan); and Tom Berghuis of Schoolcraft.

Written Materials, Vintage Photographic Images, and Professional Harness Racing Information Ellen Taylor, Chairman of the Indiana Standardbred Hall of Fame in Anderson, IN; Gail Cunard, Director of The Harness Racing Museum & Hall of Fame in Goshen, N Y; Ed Keys, Chief Photographer of the U. S. Trotting Association in Columbus, OH; Karen Greengard (Board Member) and Leann Franks of the Michigan Harness Horsemen's Association in Okemos, MI; and Nigel Soult, Photographer for The Red Mile Track, for the "Greyhound plaque" photo.

Other Photographic Images
Margie Hill, former Chairman of the Indiana Standardbred Hall of Fame; Nat Hill; and Tom Roach.

Computer Assistance
Nancy Mickenbecker; Joel Dryden (owner/manager) and Erin Harris of Bolt Graphics/The Coffee Cup; Christa Longtin; Jen Kastel for assistance in the page layout of cane photographs; and Mary Ellen De Young (especially for assistance with cover graphics).

Publishing Information, Advice, or Conversations
Larry Massie; Lynne Houghton; Nick Kekic; and April Leo.

Encouragement
Marsha Meyer; April Leo; David Motycka; Kathie Mc Connell; Pat Burlingame; Christa and Dave Longtin; Linda Dunphey; Judy Whitney; Stacy Humboldt; and Deb Secord. Special thanks to my sisters Kathy Wilson and Nancy Mickenbecker, to my daughters Jen Kastel and Kelly Motycka, to my grandson Cody, and most of all, to my husband Jim.

Introduction

There are three things you should know as you begin this story:
the first deals with the structure of the book, the second is about money,
and the third explains an unintentional riddle involving the word "article".

"Let Me Say This About That..."
The first thing I'll tell you is that you will find subheadings on each page of this book—short phrases like the bolded ones you see here—which many people will find familiar. The subheadings come from a variety of sources: titles of songs or books or movies, quotes from the same (those are sometimes printed in *italics,* as are familiar phrases or sayings), maybe riddles or deliberate plays on words—that sort of thing, all chosen to catch the eye and keep the story line flowing. If the subheading is something you recognize, well and good. Not to worry, though—if you aren't familiar with the title, quote, or whatever, you won't even realize that you've missed it, as they all still make sense to the paragraphs they introduce. Be sure to read them: they are an important part of the story, and they sometimes lead right into the text.

Show Me The Money!
The second thing is that during my research on Peter The Great, I kept coming across monetary amounts for this or that, and found myself wondering what those 1800's and early 1900's sums would equate to on today's financial scene. A short call to Ronald B. Wiser and Associates Financial Planners of Kalamazoo yielded information about an Internet website they use for such inquiries when the "comparison" years fall between 1800 and 2005. (The site was easy to use: I just inserted the amount and the years in the proper boxes, pressed "enter", and an answer appeared on the screen; calculations use the Consumer Price Index and are adjusted for inflation—check the endnotes for info.) I used the site often because doing so added a lot of depth to the story. Here's an example. If a harness horse race held in 1847 advertised winnings of $500, you might think something along the lines of "well, that's nice"—but if you find that winning that prize would be like *winning a sum of $10,000 today,* you understand its real worth.

When Is an Article Really a *Book*?
The answer is: when (in this book) I refer to anything written by John Hervey. *Why?* Because I often quoted (a great deal of the racing sequences are in his words) from the twenty–nine–page portion about Peter The Great in Hervey's classic book *The American Trotter*. Since all I ever saw of that book (which covered quite a few horses in its 551 pages) were those relatively few Xeroxed sheets, the material seemed like an article (albeit a long one) to me, so I referred to Hervey's 'article' when presenting facts. It wasn't until I mentioned Hervey's article in the epilogue that it dawned on me that it wasn't an article at all, but a book. In an attempt to be precise, I tried changing "Hervey's article" to "Hervey's book" on a few pages, but that made it sound as if Hervey had written a book about Peter The Great, which he hadn't—so I put the pages back the way they had been originally, and resolved to tell you here that the material is really from John Hervey's *book*. And now, on to Peter The Great...

Peter The Great

A horse is a horse, of course, of course—or so the saying goes.
But this horse was truly a special horse: as a young trotter, he first won fame
in harness horse racing—then went on to become one of the most
renowned sires of all time. Even today, nearly all of the
world's champion trotters carry the blood of
Peter The Great.

~~~

Born in 1895 on a horse farm that sat in the middle of the present-day
campus of Western Michigan University, the young bay colt named Peter The Great
brought distinction to the city of Kalamazoo. His owner's family home was
"The Oaklands", the stately mansion that still stands across from the
Bernhard Center—the mansion which for many years served
as home to the university's presidents.

~~~

Peter spent between three and four years of his life
right there on what would later become the campus, training
and maturing (rather like the average university student, actually).
Thousands of these students walk past a tribute to Peter The Great every day,
without even knowing it is there. It is a bronze tablet, mounted on a boulder,
inscribed with the words...but no; wait. Take up the reins,
and discover for yourself what the tablet says,
as you read on...

~~~

Part One:
The Forebears

The Darley Arabian

Messenger

Bellfounder

Jenny Lind

Hambletonian 10

Peter The Great
(Courtesy, Western Michigan University Archives and Regional History Collections)

That Thing You Do...
Kalamazoo was the birthplace of one of the most significant forefathers of a bloodline of racing horses that is unsurpassed even now—yet few of its citizens know anything about him. When he was young, Peter The Great amazed the racing world with his wins. At the age of four, he began his life's work as a sire, soon proving that he could pass along to those who came after him the heart and the desire to race, plus the athletic ability and the speed to do it—and do it well. Most of the great trotters of the twentieth century trace directly to Peter The Great, as do those of today, yet Peter The Great had to overcome adversity and abuse in his lifetime in order to achieve the fame and posterity his name so accurately foretold.[1]

To Make a Long Story (Not *Short*)—But Surely *Interesting*...

You've been told that Peter The Great was a famous horse, but you don't really know *why*. Not wanting to put the cart before the horse, (so to speak), let's go back and tell his story. Just as you can't really appreciate an acorn until, over the years, it becomes the stately tree it was meant to be, neither can you value Peter's remarkable life and legacy until you travel with him from the day he was foaled, until the sun set on the days of his greatness.

But No One Can Talk To a Horse, Of Course

...So listen to this: to find out about the life of Peter The Great, we'll have to consult sources other than Peter. We'll take some quick peeks at the history of horse racing, to get a feel for the sport, while we trace the impressive bloodlines on Peter's family tree. We'll also check out what was going on in horse racing around Kalamazoo, and explore the grounds of the estate where Peter The Great was born and raised. We'll meet him when he was a colt, discover what both his owner, and his trainer, thought of his abilities, and surprise you with his racing wins.

We'll Follow The Trail...

Then we'll follow Peter The Great's trail as his life changed with each of his three successive owners, exploring where he went to live, acknowledging the difficulties he encountered, admiring the extent of the fame he won as a sire, and visiting him where he spent his later years. We'll unearth the details of where he is buried, pinpoint where his two monuments are located, learn about some of the famous foals he sired, and get a glimpse of some of his more distant progeny (that's descendants, for the non-horse folk). So, saddle up, and let's get started.

Right Out of the Starting Gate

Now, something you need to know, right out of the starting gate, is that Peter The Great was *not* the kind of horse that raced with a jockey crouched low over his back: those are Thoroughbred horses. He was a *trotter*, a horse that was harnessed to a two-wheeled cart called a *sulky*, which has a seat from which the driver directs the horse. (There's another type of harness horse that also pulls a sulky, called a *pacer;* we'll hitch you up with an explanation of the difference between them soon.) With that bit of knowledge tucked under your hat, let's flick the reins and set off to see how long harness horse racing has been around.

Horse Racing as Far Back as Ancient Egypt, Greece, and Rome

People have been turning out to watch horse racing for ages. Peering through the mists of time, we find evidence that, in Egypt, contests were held as early as 1500 BC. In Greece, the roots of harness racing extend back to at least 680 BC, when chariot races became a part of the Olympic games. And in early Rome, chariot racing was likely the most popular and well-attended sport for entertainment: Rome's Circus Maximus, built in the 6th century BC, seated over 200,000 spectators.[2] (That was about one-quarter of the population of the city; the Romans must have been some *really* serious horse racing fans.)

 *Tracing Peter The Great's Lineage:* **The Darley Arabian (1700–1730)**

Since Peter the Great's bloodline traces back to the Thoroughbred horses of Arabia, let's take a look at what they were like. The Bedouin peoples of the unforgiving Arabian Desert depended on their horses for survival, so they bred horses that were strong, with deep chests and the good lungpower needed to get them quickly and safely across large areas of desert. And here's a surprising fact: *every* Thoroughbred is a direct descendent of three great Thoroughbred stallions of Arabian blood.[3]

~ ~ ~

The names of the three founding sires of the Thoroughbred were: the Byerly Turk, the Godolphin Arabian, and the Darley Arabian.[4] (Don't get confused here—it sounds as if these are "breeds" of horses, but they're not; they are the actual names of three individual horses.) Our particular interest lies in the last one, the Darley Arabian (whose name in Arabic was said to be *Ras el Fedowi*, meaning *the Headstrong One*),[5] who was purchased in Arabia by Thomas Darley, the British consul stationed there. The Darley Arabian was a brown stallion that stood 15 hands high, had a white face, and three white legs.[6] (One would surmise that the fourth leg was brown.) The Darley Arabian arrived in England in 1704, where he sired horses until at least 1719. This stallion was some distance back on Peter The Great's family tree.

Some Horse Terms Would Be Handy Here

Unless you know something about horses, it's already obvious that when talking about them, there are some basic terms you need to know. First, let's look at the phrase "he stood 15 hands high". A horse is measured, not in inches, but by a measurement of *hands* (a hand turned sideways), from its feet to its withers (the highest point of a horse's shoulders, where the neck and body meet). It's been done that way for many hundreds of years (after all, who had a yardstick back then?) and is still measured this way. A hand is designated as 4 inches—so a horse that stands 15 hands high (4x15) is 60 inches in height. A *sire* is a horse's father, while a *stallion,* such as the Darley Arabian, is an uncastrated male.

This Was The Start of Something Big...

How did horse racing get its start in America, eventually working its way to Kalamazoo and beyond? Early America was influenced by England in many ways: the lure of horse racing was one of them. Private wagers on two-horse races in England, very popular among the nobility, evolved into trotting races. These races became a great favorite, with large purses offered to attract the fastest horses.

~ ~ ~

Horse racing's appeal spread to the American colonies through those who came here to live. Informal races were often held on busy roads in the 1600's; by the early 1700's, formal contests had begun at racetracks.[7] Interest in harness racing waned during the stormy years of the American Revolution, but its popularity resumed as life settled down after the colonies' successful struggle for freedom came to an end. The history of the American trotter extends back to the years just following the conflict, when a great stallion named Messenger became the founding sire. (We're moving a little closer to Peter The Great on the family tree now.)

What Was That About *Purses* Attracting Horses?

No, not purses as we think of them nowadays. In Kalamazoo, as elsewhere, when horse owners talked about winning a purse, they meant winning a prize, of course. Why is it called a *purse*? There was a time when the prize money to be won in a race was placed in a purse (a small sack or bag). The purse was then hung on a wire strung across the finish line, so that, at the conclusion of the race, the rider of the horse that was farthest out in front could be seen to be literally "taking down the purse" or "going under the wire". In the old days, the purse awarded for winning a race (or for taking second, third, or fourth place) came almost entirely from the entry fees paid by the horsemen themselves. The time-honored method of 50, 25, 10 and 5 percents was usually used to split the purse among the first four horses to cross the finish line.[8] (In present-day racing, owners contribute to the purse in certain types of meets, while in other kinds they do not.)

Tracing Peter The Great's Lineage: **Messenger (1780–1808)**

Back now to Peter's bloodlines. Virtually every article about harness horse racing says that a horse named Messenger—one of Peter The Great's somewhat more recent ancestors on the family tree—was the founding sire of today's Standardbred trotters.[9] (*Standardbred?* Hold on— we'll get to that definition shortly.) Messenger's bloodlines go all the way back to those three Arabian Thoroughbred founding (or *foundation*) sires of the early 1700's, and he was a *direct* descendant of the Darley Arabian.[10] Foaled in England, Messenger raced successfully there, (even winning a race called the "King's Plate", in which horses raced carrying between 126 and 168 pounds, depending on the age of the horse). Owner Thomas Benger, an Irish sportsman, brought Messenger to America by ship, landing in Philadelphia in May of 1788. (Legend has it that the other horses were weak and ill upon their arrival, but that Messenger bounded down the gangplank of the vessel, pulling two grooms with him!) Five years later, the great Thoroughbred stallion was sold to Henry Astor of New York, (brother of wealthy fur trader John Jacob Astor). Henry Astor, in turn, sold Messenger in 1796 to Cornelius Van Ranst.

~ ~ ~

Messenger was a gray stallion of superb form, with amazing power and spirit; he had strong loins, powerful hindquarters, and stood a bit over 15 hands high. And he had an unusual ability: Messenger was able to sire both fast Thoroughbreds *and* fast trotters. His ability to sire large, powerfully built horses known for their trotting form, their speed, and their gameness was unequaled.[11] Before long, Messenger's descendants dominated the racecourses of the nation.[12] (Praise of Peter The Great's abilities, over a century later, would echo those words.) Used as a sire until 1807, Messenger produced about a thousand offspring during his twenty years standing at stud in America, before he died at the age of twenty-eight on January 28, 1808.[13] Looking at the family tree, we see that Messenger was Peter's four-times great-grandfather; the relationship is traced through Peter's dam.

"Dam"—That Word Needs Some Explanation; So Does "Stud"

The word *dam* means a horse's mother. A *stud* is a male kept primarily for the purpose of breeding, while *standing at stud* means, apparently, just that: the stallion is available for breeding services. And *stud fees* (a phrase that we'll encounter soon) are fees set by the stallion's owner for the breeding services provided by the stallion.

A Definition of a "Standardbred" Horse Would Definitely Help Here...

So, Messenger was the founding sire of the Standardbred horse. But just what does the word *Standardbred* mean? To find out, we have to jump our horses over nearly a century (from the time Messenger was born), and land briefly in 1879. That was the year the National Association of Trotting Horse Breeders agreed to set a "standard" time of 2:30 for a distance of one mile. Simply put, only horses that could trot or pace one mile in two-and-a-half minutes or less—and that was considered pretty fast in those days—were eligible to be included in John H. Wallace's *Trotting Register*, which recorded the pedigrees of horses. (The actual use of the name *Standardbred* would come along sometime later.)

"Believe Me Or Believe Me Not..."

Messenger is called the founding sire of Standardbred horses because, believe it or not, *all* Standardbreds have descended from his bloodline. Of course, horse owners back when that standard was set certainly wanted to have their fastest horses included in Wallace's register. Today, the standard is a bit more rigid, having been reduced to 2:20 for two-year olds and 2:15 for older horses.[14] Although the standard times were changed to make them more challenging, horses have continued to get even faster over the years (just as our human marathon runners have). Horse owners today say that racing times would really have to be 1:55 to 2:00 to be competitive. But we're getting ahead of ourselves now, so let's jump back over the hurdle, and return to the 19th century.

Tracing Peter The Great's Lineage: **Bellfounder (1815-1843)**

Peter The Great had another ancestor who, while not nearly as well known as Messenger, was also mentioned in one article as a source in the bloodlines of the American trotter, so we'll include him in our lineage lineup, too.[15] Bellfounder, foaled in 1815, also traveled by ship from England; he arrived in America in 1822, when he was seven years old. In the region of Orange County, New York where he was brought to live, he was regarded as one of the fastest and most powerful trotters of his time.

~ ~ ~

Bellfounder was a bright bay that stood 15 hands high, a "natural trotter", said to have been able to trot 17 miles in an hour. Bellfounder went into stud service when he arrived in New York, and sired a great many horses (although records did not indicate how many). Bellfounder died in Long Island, New York in 1843, at the age of twenty-eight.[16] A close look at the family tree shows that Bellfounder was Peter's great-great-grandfather on his sire's side.

Hope This Isn't Biting Off More Than You Can Chew...

The remarkable stallions on Peter The Great's family tree certainly sired their share of offspring, and in the early days of Kalamazoo, nearly everyone would have known the right horse terms to use for those offspring. We don't want you to buck if you encounter a word that you are uncertain about, so here are a few more terms, starting right where nature does: with the babies. A baby horse still at its mother's side is called a *foal*, and the place where it was born is where it was *foaled*. Another term, *yearling,* is a bit tricky: in racing, it means a horse in its second calendar year of life, beginning on January 1 of the year following when it was foaled. (Most of us will need to read that definition again, to really catch its meaning.) A foal can be just one day old and be a yearling, if it was born on December 31.

Let's Get *Sulk*y For Just a Minute Here

Trainers in those days rode in a sulky named, it is said, because long ago the wife of a driver who made a one-man cart (so he could drive alone) referred to him as a "sulky" kind of man. In 1823, the first official trotting races in America were held at the Union Course in Long Island, New York. A North-South challenge held there that year drew an astounding 60,000 spectators to a contest featuring three four-mile heats, (we'll fill you in later on what "heats" are), between two horses.[17] At the time, horses pulled carts that weighed roughly 108 pounds, measured over nine feet long, and had wheels approximately five feet in diameter. By the 1850's, sulky weight had been reduced to about 70-75 pounds; today's sulky weight averages about 35-40 pounds.[18]

~ ~ ~

Nearly three decades would pass before the first bent-axle sulky hit the market in 1878; this improvement brought the sulky closer to the horse, which reduced both wind resistance and slew on bends.[19] When driving the sulky, the trainer carried a long, light whip, which was mostly used to signal the horse by striking or tapping the sulky shaft to make noise. (Incidentally, the *sound* of a whip cracking seems to occur *after* the motion because, when used by an experienced trainer, the tip of the whip can move faster than the speed of sound.)

Tracing Peter The Great's Lineage: **Jenny Lind (1845-?)**

Now we'll meet Peter's great-grandmother, Jenny Lind, daughter of the horse Bellfounder. *Whoa!* Hold up a minute—say that again? It's true: closer now on the family tree was a horse named Jenny Lind, who was Peter The Great's great-grandam. (We're not horsing around about this: the foal was named for the Swedish singer who was wildly popular in the United States at the time.) Using human terms to explain the relationship to Peter in an easier fashion, here we go: Jenny Lind would have a daughter named Tackey (also known as Polly) who was "a great race mare that could go any distance". Tackey would have a son named Pilot Medium, who, exactly half a century after Jenny Lind had been born, would have a son of his own: the foal's name would be Peter The Great.[20]

~ ~ ~

Jenny Lind was a fast horse for her time. Entered in a three-heat race at the Union Course (this Union course was located near New Orleans) on November 17, 1847, with the one-mile heats matched for $500 (a purse worth over $10,000 in today's money)[21], Jenny Lind won the second and fastest heat, beating her opponent, Black Hawk, with a time of 2:38. This very race, and those two horses, had the honor of being depicted in a Currier & Ives lithograph hand-colored way back in 1850. That lithograph (which features both horses pulling their drivers in the sulkies used in the competition) is still in good condition, and was recently up for sale with an asking price of $2,750.[22]

Now, Hold Your Horses (And They Often Did In Kalamazoo)
The actual harness racing with which many people are familiar today began about fifteen years before Jenny Lind was foaled, and was derived from the custom of the informal carriage races we touched on earlier. By the time Jenny Lind was racing as a two-year old, Kalamazoo's first horse racing track had already been operating for a decade. The Burr Oak Track (also known as the Axtell Track) had opened back in 1837 near the southwest section of the village, west of Westnedge and south of Vine Street.[23] The track was in operation for just over twenty years (closing in 1858, the same year the second track opened). Around this time, roughly the mid-1850's, driving contests at state and county fairs grew increasingly popular.

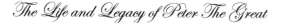 *Tracing Peter The Great's Lineage:* **Hambletonian 10 (1849-1876)**
Edging closer on the family tree to Peter The Great, we now meet Hambletonian 10, great-grandson of the renowned Messenger.[24] While Messenger has long been hailed as the founding sire from whom all Standardbreds have descended, many in the harness racing world today would say that it is Hambletonian 10 that has actually come to be best known as the true founding sire of the Standardbred. The reason? Hambletonian 10 sired four sons (including Happy Medium, the grandsire of Peter The Great) who themselves became great sires. Through those four sons a virtual sovereignty was established, so that an estimated 99% of all American Standardbred racehorses trace back through them to Hambletonian 10: he is considered to be the greatest progenitor (forefather)—and the most celebrated horse—in all of American harness racing history.

~ ~ ~

As a foal, Hambletonian 10 had an inauspicious start: both he and his dam were sold to a farm hand named William Rysdyk for a total price of $125. (Rysdyk had become very fond of the foal, and implored the owner to be allowed to purchase the pair.) Rysdyk's roughly two-year old colt soon caught the eye of local horsemen at a county fair, and he was challenged to race at the Union Course in New York; when the colt won the meet by a very considerable seven seconds (with a time of 2:48½), the interest generated was so high that he was started at stud soon after.[25] Time passed, and the brilliant performances of the colts Hambletonian 10 sired brought the horse fame near and far; considered the leading "speed" sire for many years, his stud fees eventually earned Rysdyk over $200,000.[26] (A huge amount at the time, comparable to over $3 million today.) No one could have known it then, but the course of harness racing had been set for all time in 1849—on the day Hambeltonian 10 was foaled in Orange County, New York.[27]

~ ~ ~

Hambletonian 10 was a mahogany bay; his head was large, with a small white star above pleasant eyes. He was a horse of powerful build with massive quarters and a great chest, a horse whose impressive stature earned him the nickname "Rysdyk's Big Bull".[28] Hambletonian 10 stood 15½ hands high[29], and was taller at the rump than he was in front; in fact, he passed on this downhill conformation, called the "trotting pitch", to many of his offspring. He had black legs (his legs and feet were described as being "superior in character") with white hind ankles. Hambletonian 10, who sired 1,331 foals, died in 1876 at the age of twenty-six. Peter The Great, who would be born almost half a century later, was Hambletonian 10's great-grandson on his dam's side.

Go Straight To The Source and Ask The Horse...

We know something about the history of the Standardbred now, and that nearly all Standardbreds trace back to the four sons of Hambletonian 10. The Standardbred resembles its Thoroughbred ancestors in many respects, but with two distinct differences. Now let's find out just what this breed of horse looks like.[30] If a Standardbred horse could talk, it would tell you that the first difference between it and a Thoroughbred is that a Standardbred's head is bigger, yet is typically well proportioned: refined, straight and chiseled, with a broad forehead, shallow mouth, and small muzzle. Standardbreds might have what is called a "Roman nose" (a slight bulge beneath the eyes which continues until it reaches the nose) and large nostrils. Its ears ("the better to hear you with, my dear") are generally medium to small in size and widely set, its eyes often large and clear, reflecting its calm nature. The Standardbred would tell you, too, that its neck is slightly arched, lean and muscular; it has long, sloping, strong shoulders, and a deep and thick chest.

"And Not Only That..."

The second difference is that Standardbreds are considerably longer in body and more muscled than their Thoroughbred ancestors—but not as tall. (In fact, many Standardbreds are actually *longer* than they are tall, and have proportionately shorter legs than a Thoroughbred does.) Since Peter The Great and his descendents are all Standardbred horses, let's not wait any longer to take a look at the typical body size and build of this breed of horse. Generally speaking, a Standardbred is of medium build, roughly 14 to 17 hands in height, and somewhere around 900 to 1200 pounds in weight. Its muscling is heavy and long, allowing its long fluid stride. The Standardbred is the fastest racing breed in harness, robust and rugged, with great stamina; this honest, tractable, and steady horse is capable of performing just about any job it is given, and excels both on and off the racetrack.[31] Now we have an excellent idea of the Standardbred as to its appearance, but we haven't added color to the picture yet.

"Black Beauty"

The phrase "black beauty" can mean, of course, a horse with a glossy black coat, but—we're going to lead you off track here for just a second, as this is quite interesting—we want to tell you that it can also refer to the title of a classic children's book published nearly two decades before Peter The Great was born. The story, *written by the horse in its own words*, described the good treatment—and the cruelty—the gentle horse had received at the hands of his various owners. We'll also tell you that the book had a tremendous impact on the public: great strides were made in establishing better treatment of horses. Now, let's get back to color. Black is just one of the colors that a Standardbred horse can be: other colors are chestnut, bay, brown, and occasionally gray without spots or patches. And back in the early days, horses of all colors and sizes could be seen in the bustling streets of Kalamazoo.

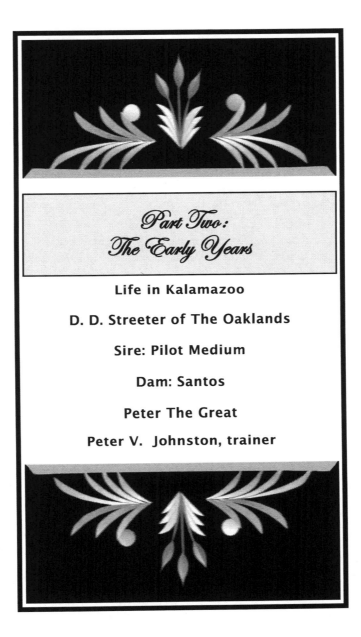

Part Two:
The Early Years

Life in Kalamazoo

D. D. Streeter of The Oaklands

Sire: Pilot Medium

Dam: Santos

Peter The Great

Peter V. Johnston, trainer

Kalamazoo's Race Street and Race *Tracks*

Trotting right along, we learn that the first Standardbred contests were raced on—to put it simply—just *streets*, with men challenging friends to see who had the fastest horse. Streets in major cities were often closed just long enough to have a race conducted on them, which is why so many American cities have a street called "Race" Street. Kalamazoo was no exception: its Race Street is located east of Portage Road, running north and south between Palmer and Hays Park. But did the citizens of Kalamazoo also hold impromptu horse races along Race Street? Or was it named that because of its proximity to Kalamazoo's second racetrack? (Or another reason altogether?) The answer is lost in time...

~ ~ ~

In 1858, the National Driving Park opened in the Hays Park section of Washington Square. When the park closed about 1886, the city of Kalamazoo went without a racetrack for almost twenty years. (There were other racetracks in Kalamazoo County, however, including one in the village of Schoolcraft, situated on land near an area where several sets of train tracks come close together.) Kalamazoo's third and last racetrack, Recreation Park (now the fair grounds on Lake Street, east of the city of Kalamazoo) was built in 1903. The last of the area's Grand Circuit races were held at Recreation Park in 1931, which effectively ended serious horse racing in the city of Kalamazoo. (But we've raced too far ahead here; let's get back again to the 1870's.)

Sam Browne's Stock Farm

Where did Kalamazooans go when they wanted to buy a horse? Odds are they went on over to see Sam Browne on the west side of town. Scotch-Irishman Samuel A. Browne had started out in the horse business at nearby Pentwater, and by 1875 was traveling in search of good broodmares for his farm. One of the many high-priced horses purchased by Browne (whose wealth came in part from his lumber camps in the Muskegon area) was a mare named Lady Duncan, for whom he paid $3,000[32] (a large sum to pay back then for any horse; that would be a price of around $60,000 nowadays). Browne switched the mare's name to Shadow and tried her as a racehorse, but found her temperamental and thus not suited to racing.

~ ~ ~

In the 1880's and the years leading up to the turn of the century, Browne owned and operated the Kalamazoo Stock Farm, a nearly 240-acre tract of land situated east of Drake Road on the south side of West Main Street (now the location of Kalsec, Inc).[33] Harness racing had become very popular during the past few decades, and the sandy-haired Browne was well known in "horse" circles. Browne's Stock Farm was one of the best horse breeding establishments in Michigan; it was also the largest Standardbred nursery in the state at the close of the 19th century.[34] Browne sold horses to many people, including wealthy Kalamazoo railroad man Daniel D. Streeter, a man, it was said, who "knew horses". In 1891, Browne would sell Streeter a mare named Santos (a daughter of Shadow) who, just a few years later, would bear a foal named Peter The Great.

15

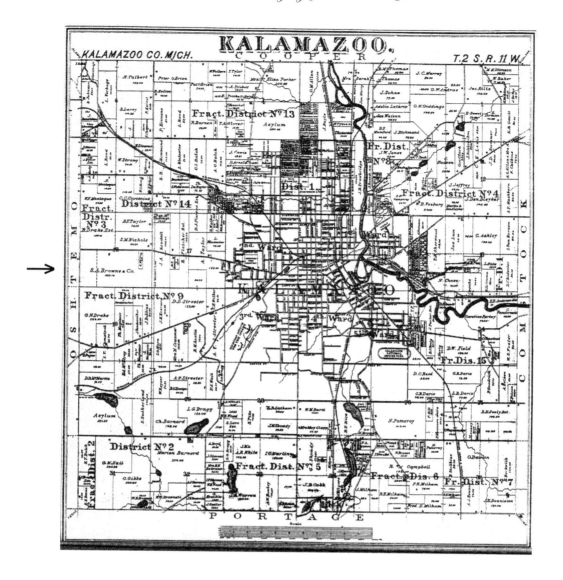

A close look at this 1890's map shows the "S. A. Browne & Co." parcel (adjacent to left margin, about halfway down) on West Main Street in Kalamazoo. (Courtesy, Western Michigan University Archives and Regional History Collections)

Sex In The City (Referring, Naturally, To Horse Gender)

Of the many foals that were sired in the city, (Kalamazoo became a city in 1884), at places like Browne's, some were of course male, some female. So, as we're going to meet Peter The Great's dam soon, we'll concentrate on gender and introduce a few more horse terms here. Since the youngest horses have already been tended to, we'll do the ladies first: a *filly* is a female horse under four years old, while a *mare* is a female horse over the age of four; a *broodmare* is a female horse that is used strictly for breeding. (What's the gestation period for a mare? It's eleven months, and most births are single; females are not usually spayed. And by the way, the average lifespan of a horse is 20–25 years, although 30 is said to be fairly common.) Now for the gentlemen: a *colt* is an uncastrated male under four years old, a *stallion* is a male horse over the age of four, and a *gelding* is a male horse that has been castrated (or "fixed", as the non-horse person might say). Now that we have these terms under control, let's head out south of the city, and meet the man who will be the owner of Peter The Great.

Streeter Was a Horse Breeder
Wealthy railroad man Daniel Denison Streeter was a breeder of horses, so he knew horse terms well. Described as a "railroad builder and contractor of big railroad grading operations", Streeter was also said to be involved in land development. According to R. A. Patton of the *Kalamazoo Gazette* in an article written in 1944, those who knew the man said that when Streeter was in Chicago during the week, he drove himself hard to accumulate wealth with his railroad work, but that he was a horseman, and "when he was at his Oaklands home here, horses unquestionably came first".[35] Streeter, with his passion for horses, brought much attention to The Oaklands by turning its green pastures into a breeding farm for harness racers. Before long, Streeter would buy Peter The Great's dam-to-be, Santos, from Sam Browne, and move her to his horse farm south of Kalamazoo. Let's ride out for a look at the land, find out about the previous owners of the estate, and then meet the Streeter family.

A Jewel Set In Green Velvet: 'The Oaklands' of Kalamazoo
The young city of Kalamazoo was much smaller in those days, so the land was aptly described as a 600-acre farm situated "south of the city", right above the Territorial Road (now called Stadium Drive). The jewel of the estate was a beautiful Italianate villa, nestled amongst the oak trees at the center of the farm. The villa, which cost $15,000 to build (comparable to over $200,000 now) still stands today, right across Michigan Avenue from the Bernhard Center of Western Michigan University. Are you familiar with the spot? Try to imagine the land as it must have been in the days before the university was built: rolling hills covered with waving grasses in many shades of green and dotted with wildflowers, with a dirt road running out from the heart of the city and winding its way up to the red brick home set on one of those hills. Topped with an ornate cupola, the majestic twenty-three room mansion (called 'The Oaklands' for the trees in its front yard) had luxuries such as a beautiful circular staircase, servants' quarters, a walk-in icebox, and a butler's pantry. The Oaklands stands—more than a century after Peter The Great was born—a subtle testimony to the grace and elegance of those long ago days.

The Oaklands
(Used with the permission of the KALAMAZOO GAZETTE)

Origins of The Oaklands...
The Oaklands was erected in 1869 by Robert S. Babcock (a businessman and seller of dry goods who would later become head of the new First National Bank) because he "wanted to become a country gentleman".[36] In 1873, Babcock sold the luxurious mansion and estate to Benjamin M. Austin, a wagon builder, investor, and developer. Two years after the purchase, the new owner established the Austin Hersey Dairy Farm[37] on the green pastures adjacent to The Oaklands—the same pastures that would later become a horse farm. Austin and his wife had a daughter, Amelia, who grew from a child into a young woman while at The Oaklands. Time passed; Amelia met and married successful railroad builder Daniel Streeter, and the couple established a home in Chicago.

"Come Back?"

Amelia's father, finding both the farm and the mansion more demanding of his time than he wanted, asked his daughter and her family to move back from Chicago to The Oaklands and to make the estate their home. Streeter accepted his father-in-law's invitation, and the move was made. Daniel and Amelia had two daughters, Fannie and Blanche, who soon filled the family home with excitement and vitality as they shared good times with their friends. Roughly two decades after Austin's original purchase, Streeter accepted ownership of the estate where Peter The Great would soon be foaled. The villa at the center of the estate had always been a place of gracious living and hospitality; with the addition of the Streeter family, it would remain so for some time to come.

Framed portrait of Daniel D. Streeter
(Courtesy, Western Michigan University Archives and Regional History Collections)

"He Loved His Horses..."

Streeter liked watching the trains that raced by the grounds of the estate (on tracks that followed the route of the Territorial Road), trains that puffed clouds of smoke that lingered for a while after the train itself had disappeared—and he took those trains many times to Chicago for work. Driven by the demands of his business, he found the estate in Kalamazoo to be both "his refuge and his delight", according to R. A. Patton in the *Kalamazoo Gazette* article mentioned earlier. Streeter's great love for and good treatment of his horses was well known; he even built a two-story barn (with an elevator running between floors), and installed fresh running water for the horses.[38] (Several years before it was installed in the house, as a matter of fact: wonder what his wife thought about *that?*)

~ ~ ~

Streeter planted a line of trees—he called it Arbor Day Drive—along the bottom of a nearby hill, beside a spot that was a favorite of his: the paddock for his horses and broodmares. Streeter would often say, "When I go...I'd like to be buried here on the green under the trees, where I can hear the trains go by, and be near my horses", Patton related in the *Gazette* article. This was the pastoral setting in which Peter The Great would soon be foaled and would spend his early years. By then both daughters had become young women in their twenties, and both were married. Before long, the mansion rang with the laughter of grandchildren. When Streeter heard of the youngsters' wish for a playhouse, Patton tells us, their grandfather had a log cabin built for them, east of the mansion, tucked amongst the trees on the estate.

"Meet The Parents"

Sire: *Dam:*
Pilot Medium   **Santos**

Peter The Great's Sire: Pilot Medium (1879-1896)
After studying racing journals, a young banker from Battle Creek by the name of Walter Clark took a trip out east to buy some horses. Stopping in Pennsylvania, he purchased Pilot Medium (son of Happy Medium, one of Hambletonian 10's four famous sons) for $125. As a yearling, Pilot Medium had suffered an accident that left him with a bad hip, so Clark planned to use the lame two-year old colt strictly as a sire on his modest breeding farm; stud fees were set at $75.[39] Since Pilot Medium could not race, his capacity for speed was obviously unknown; not considered a top sire, he was not booked to the best mares. Yet Pilot Medium, grandson of Hambletonian 10,[40] would surprise many who followed horse racing by siring a lot of fast foals.

~ ~ ~

Pilot Medium was a gray horse that stood 16 hands high. He had what was called an "Arabian head", described as "one of real beauty, finely chiseled, triangular in shape, with a small fine muzzle and fine thin lips". Horses with a head described as Arabian often have nostrils that are delicately curled, large eyes that tend to be set far apart, and very flexible, upright pointed ears.[41] Pilot Medium would die when he was just seventeen; the colt he sired with Santos, Peter The Great, would be just a yearling at the time.

~ ~ ~

Over half a century after Pilot Medium's death, in his book *The American Trotter*, well-respected trotting historian John Hervey described Pilot Medium as Michigan's "greatest sire" (of the day).[42] More praise for Pilot Medium came at the end of the twentieth century, when an article published by Karen Greengard in the *Michigan Harness Horseman* described him as "one of the most successful trotting sires [of his time] in the country".[43] Pilot Medium had been standing at stud for roughly thirteen years when Santos, who would be Peter's dam, was sent from the Streeter farm in Kalamazoo to Battle Creek to be bred.

Peter The Great's Dam: Santos (1887-1916)

In the winter of 1891, Daniel Streeter bought four-year old Santos from Sam Browne for $1,000 (a purchase price equal to over $20,000 today). Santos was a great-granddaughter of Hambletonian 10 on her sire's side, and her paternal lineage was clear. Her origins on her dam's side, however, were said to be "somewhat obscure", as one of her maternal great-granddams was unknown. In years to come, Santos would be sharply criticized about that missing piece of information. Yet uncertainties about Santos' bloodlines were largely disproved as the years passed, says that same *Michigan Harness Horseman* article, as both she—and her dam—*each* produced four well-known (trotting) performers. Furthering the speculations that the unknown ancestor might have been of good breeding, the article went on to say, was the fact that, more than half a century after Peter The Great was born, Santos remained the *sole* mare that had ever borne two sons (one of whom was Peter The Great) that *both* became sires of over one hundred record performers.[44] Santos had borne only one prior foal, when in 1894, at the age of seven, she was sent to Battle Creek to be bred with Pilot Medium. The result was Peter The Great.

~ ~ ~

Santos, a medium-sized brown mare with no white markings, had a smooth and straight head and neck, a long body, and rather short legs. Santos herself was not very fast (in fact, Streeter once tried to sell her to an acquaintance, who actually refused her for that reason) yet she was the sister of four high-class trotters with fine racing records.[45] (Worthy of note here is one of Santos' ancestors, a Thoroughbred mare named Lady Bess that had been in fighting during the Civil War with her owner, a regiment cavalry officer from Louisiana.[46] Horses played a major part in warfare, where steadiness and dependability was required in the midst of the thunder of musket fire, the clash of steel bayonets, and the screams of wounded men and horses.)

~ ~ ~

Santos, who was twenty years old when she bore the last of her nine foals in 1907, was never sold again: she spent her remaining days in comfort on the grounds of The Oaklands. Daniel Streeter must have had a special place in his heart for the dam of Peter The Great. Prior to his death on September 28, 1909, Streeter had directed that when he died, all of his horses were to be sold at the Old Glory sale in New York, except for one: Santos. Pensioned off by the estate, Santos finished out her days, content on the Streeter farm in Kalamazoo, until she died in 1916, at the age of twenty-nine. Santos was buried on the grounds of The Oaklands, behind the barn where she had borne her famous foal.

"Now, Wilbur..."

Right across the road from Streeter's horse farm stood the Wilbur Home and School for the Feeble-Minded, a private institution for children considered mentally deficient. The institution (which had opened in 1884, seven years before Santos' arrival at The Oaklands) provided a home environment for those whose parents could afford a private facility. Located where several of the university's buildings stand today (the Bernhard Center, and Ellsworth, Hoekje, Henry, and Bigelow Halls) the Wilbur Home was in operation for over sixty years. The presence of the horses at the neighboring Streeter farm may have been good for the children living at the Home, as present-day medicine tells us about the calming and stress-relieving effects of animals. Now let's cross the dirt road back over to The Oaklands, make our way to the Streeter barn, open the door, and step inside—straight into the year 1895.

We've Traced The Lineage All The Way Now To:

Peter The Great (1895-1923)

"All The Right Stuff"

Although no one would have expected Peter's parentage to be "all the right stuff", right it certainly proved to be. We've learned about some of the prestigious ancestors of Peter The Great, the most recent of which was Hambletonian 10, the founding father of the Standardbreds. (A close look shows that Peter The Great is related to Hambletonian 10 through *both* of his parents, as Hambletonian 10 is the great-grandsire of Peter The Great on his paternal side, and is also Peter's great-*great* grandsire on his maternal side.) We have met Peter's sire, Pilot Medium, and know that, although crippled, he came to be known as the most successful sire of his day in Michigan. And we have met Peter's dam, Santos, learned about the doubts of the bloodlines on her maternal side, and learned that they greatly dimmed with the passage of time.

~ ~ ~

And thus we come to Peter The Great, who was born in 1895. Who could have guessed, watching the little bay foal struggle shakily to his feet for the first time, that Peter The Great would rise like a shooting star for a brief but brilliant racing career—a career that would bring fame to his owner, Daniel Streeter...to his trainer, Peter V. Johnston...and to the city of Kalamazoo. No one could have predicted then that, following in the steps of his forebears, Peter The Great would one day become an eminent foundation sire in his own right, a horse well able to pass both his trotting power and his staying power to his progeny, progeny who, in the years ahead, would come to dominate the breed of trotting horses.[47]

"You Say It's Your Birthday..."

So, what day was Peter The Great's *birthday?* Efforts to determine Peter's actual birth-date were unsuccessful. Since the date could not be found, the Harness Racing Museum & Hall of Fame in Goshen, New York offered the general information that horses are often foaled in the spring. (Nature generally provides excellent grass in the spring and early summer months, which helps the dam's milk supply.) For simplicity in horse racing, most foals are simply given the birth-date of January 1 in the year in which they were born. (It appears that, until a horse becomes famous, the actual birth-date is unimportant; by contrast, once the horse *has* become famous, the date of death is usually quite easy to find, as people are of course interested.) Now we're off to find out what Peter looked like. Turf historian John Hervey has provided us with the following description of Peter the Great, in the prime of his life, which just can't be beat...[48]

"A Horse of a *Different* Color"

Reminiscent of the line about a "horse of a different color" (in the beloved movie classic in which there's no place like home), Peter The Great's bay coat was "different" and difficult to define—which is why he was often simply called "brown". You'd almost have to be a wizard to decipher the meaning of the term "bay", as it can indicate a color anywhere from a yellowish tan, called "light bay", all the way to a dark shade of mahogany. Peter The Great, who stood 16 hands high, was described as a "rich blood bay", a reddish-brown bay, with a coat that Hervey tells us was "beautiful in both color and texture" with "black points" (shadings of black), in a coat that was short, fine, and with "the gloss and glow of satin". His foretop (the hair standing up over his eyes) was "rather light" in color, as were his mane and tail. His tail was short and "set on rather high", with "its fringes dropping but little below his hocks". (Non-horse people can easily identify the hock, a joint located roughly half way down the rear leg, as it looks something like a knee pointing backwards.)

21

Peter The Great
(Courtesy, U. S. Trotting Association)

"I Never Met Another Horse Like You..."

Hervey, who knew the horse quite well, pens a wonderful description of Peter's appearance. Yet, in almost the same breath, he acknowledges that Peter The Great was not a horse that remained always "admirable and even handsome", but that he "varied astonishingly at various periods of his career". At times Peter "appeared very common–looking and unattractive", says Hervey, and there were times when "he appeared a splendid specimen of the Standard breed", depending on his condition at the time. Hervey goes on to describe Peter The Great as having a "plain but very intelligent" head (rather large than small), with a "small [white] star between his eyes, narrow and pointed". (His only other markings were towards the bottom of his left hind leg, which was white in front, and which also had a white spot on the outside, farther down.) Peter's head was "Roman in profile", with eyes that were "not large but luminous and expressive", and ears a "trifle broad but well carried", and his neck was "of good length".

And He Had Great Legs...

Hervey assures us that Peter The Great had an "appearance [that] was in keeping with his achievements", and his eloquent words continue: Peter's "point of superiority", he states, was his "body, hips, quarters and stifles" (stifles are the next joint above the hock, similar to a knee in a human) and "it would be difficult", says Hervey, his words reflecting both admiration and pride, "to find a horse of any breed, including a Thoroughbred of the highest type"...so "magnificent". Peter was "longer than he was tall" and was "superbly 'furnished'...across the loin". His "grandeur" of hind quarter "had to be seen to be appreciated" with a "depth, fullness, roundness, and symmetry" of proportions, "rarely" seen in the Standardbred, but observed occasionally among Thoroughbreds. Peter's "forearm was powerful, but the muscles were long and shapely", the tendons in his forelegs "cleanly defined", his legs "naturally of fine form and texture". And now, having seen what Peter The Great looked like when he was grown up and in excellent condition, we must go back—and meet him when he was foaled.

22

"Were You Born In a Barn?"

(A question frequently asked by human mothers.) As a matter of fact, he was: he was foaled in the frame barn at The Oaklands. Peter The Great, at first not straying far from his dam's side, would soon try out his legs in the paddock not far from the oak trees on Arbor Day Drive. Before long, he was frisking and galloping around the field with the other colts, kicking up his legs—in short, doing all of the things that young horses will do. Peter was described as a "leggy brown colt" by Jud Graine, a stableman at The Oaklands, who also said the colt was "spirited and gentle as a kitten...often nuzzling for sugar", according to the *Kalamazoo Gazette*.[49] Seasons changed, and the foal—now a yearling—grew under the watchful eyes of his owner, and those of the trainer Streeter had chosen for the colt, a man by the name of Peter V. Johnston. Streeter felt that with Peter The Great's breeding, the colt just might be a good racehorse. With that in mind, he instructed Johnston to "make a Futurity [one of horse racing's most prestigious races for two–year olds] colt out of him".[50] Johnston, known as one of the best trainers in the business, would in fact do just that. Let's circle the rails of the paddock now, and meet the trainer for ourselves.

"Hoofing It"

Peter V. Johnston, born in Marshall, Michigan in 1842, made his living shoeing horses.[51] He operated a public stable in Chicago for a bit, then realized he could make more money training and driving horses. Around 1885, he became a private trainer for Sam Browne at Browne's Stock farm in Kalamazoo,[52] and trained horses for Daniel Streeter for a number of years. Streeter had a high regard for Johnston, who was considered to be at the top of Michigan's trainers and drivers.[53] (Such high regard, in fact, that on Streeter's deathbed some years later, in September of 1909, he would give Johnston the right to choose—as his gift—any horse the trainer wished to select from the Streeter stables, said the *Gazette*.)[54]Streeter's esteem for Johnston in fact prompted him to name the new colt "Peter The Great" after the trainer (not after the Russian czar, as many had mistakenly thought). When the colt was thought to be ready for training, Streeter asked Johnston to break Peter The Great in, train him to trot, and drive him in races when the time came.

He Chose *Wisely*

Johnston was described as a man of medium height and powerful build, a determined and skilled driver who "sat erect, had his horse in control at all times", and was "one of the best" of the outstanding drivers and trainers of the past.[55] The white-haired Johnston, fifty-three years old when Peter The Great was foaled, had been about to retire and go on a long fishing trip when Streeter (just one year younger) asked him to take on the responsibilities of Peter The Great's training. Eventually, persuaded by the persistent owner, Johnston agreed to do so. (One article said Johnston might have housed the colt for a time in a small barn in back of his own home; a much later article gave Johnston's address as 719 S. Westnedge Avenue.)[56] Johnston's work with Peter The Great would later on help the trainer earn a niche in the Driving Hall of Fame—but training Peter The Great to trot, he soon found, would not be an easy task.[57]

Foal Facts

We'll fold in some facts on foals for you here: Within an hour or so after birth, a newborn foal is able to struggle to a standing position on wobbly legs, so that it can feed from its mother's milk. The foal gains strength at first just from this; by about eight weeks, the foal adds grass to its menu.

~ ~ ~

At around four months, a foal (with legs now strong and sturdy) sheds its milk hairs and grows an adult coat. A foal is weaned (stops taking milk from its mother) when it is roughly five to six months old; it might then be called a *weanling*.

Peter V. Johnston
(Used with the permission of the KALAMAZOO GAZETTE)

Part Three:
The Racing Years

Racing with Streeter of Kalamazoo

The Futurities

Sold to J. Malcolm Forbes

Racing with Forbes of Boston

Life at Forbes' Farm

Put Your Right Foot Forward, and Your Left Foot...

Back? Not necessarily. Let's rein in for just a minute here, and learn about the way a trotter moves his feet in a race, in a movement called the *trotter's gait.* Why learn about this? Because (although the trotting gait is not unnatural in the animal world) some horses are *natural* trotters, and some are not. And, although Peter The Great would thrill the racing world with his wins, he was one of the *"nots"*: Peter had a hard time learning how to trot. Here's how the trotting gait works. (If Peter could learn it, so can we.) A trotter's gait is one in which the horse's *foreleg* moves in tandem with the *opposite hind leg,* (for instance, the right front and left rear legs move forward at the same time). Sounds tricky, doesn't it? It requires much skill by the trainer to get a trotter to be well balanced and moving perfectly, front to back, at high speeds. (A *pacer,* the other type of harness horse, also pulls a sulky, but has a different gait. Called a *pacer's gait,* it is one in which the horse's foreleg moves in tandem with the rear leg on the *same side* when moving forward; for instance, the right front and right rear legs move forward at the same time. Distinctly unlike the trotter's gait, the pacer's gait is also a bit faster.) Now, give those reins a flick, and let's catch up with Peter, as Johnston begins working with him.

One Is Too Heavy, One Is Too Light: This One is Juuust Right

Johnston broke the yearling (got him used to wearing a bit, bridle, and harness, and to pulling a cart behind him) in the fall of 1896, worked with him for about a month, then halted training for the winter. From the beginning, Johnston found Peter The Great a difficult horse to train—Peter just couldn't manage his feet going fast, as his gait was mixed and uneven. When Johnston started back with the colt in the spring of 1897, he found that it wouldn't have taken much prompting for his pupil to be a pacer; but the trainer persevered with the trotter's gait, as Streeter had said he definitely wanted a trotter.[58] Johnston discovered that the only way he could get Peter properly balanced, and able to hold his stride when up to speed at a trot, was to use heavy iron shoes on his front feet. Horseshoes, always worn to protect the horse's hooves from breaking on rough or rocky ground, could be a great asset in racing when additional weight was added. *Why?* The extra weight curbed Peter's tendency to swing his front leg out to the side as he brought it around while trotting, thus it gave his stride more forward momentum. Drawing on his years and skills at horseshoeing, Johnston had become an expert "twenty years ahead of his time at the art of balancing trotters with weighted shoes", to quote a statement by turf writer Ten Eyck White in the *Kalamazoo Gazette.*[59] Now he would decide how much weight was too much for Peter to manage, how much was too little to make a difference, and how much was just right. Johnston also fitted Peter with toe weights, so that altogether the horse sometimes carried as much as twenty ounces in extra weight on each front foot.[60]

You Can Lead a Horse To Water, But You Can't Make Him—*Trot?*

What Peter The Great had learned about how to trot during those four weeks the previous autumn, he had promptly forgotten over the winter: he had to learn it all over again. Also, like his dam, he showed no burst of speed. Peter The Great did not look "great" at all. As June came, and the time for payment to hold a spot in the Kentucky Futurity (the prestigious race we mentioned before, to be held that fall) drew near, Peter, in spite of training day after day, was still not fast enough. And, although Streeter very much wanted to enter him in the race, he really doubted whether he should. Finally one day, Streeter, in effect, did what all parents often do: he decided to give the colt just *one last opportunity* to prove himself—or Peter's chance at the race would be off. Perhaps sensing his owner's resolve, and with the supreme efforts of his trainer, the colt—just barely—came up with enough speed that day to show Streeter that he could do it, and the payment was made.[61]

27

Today, They've "New and Improved" It...

Of course, over the years, things have changed. Around the 1950's, a vehicle took the place of the official holding the white flag. Most harness races today start from behind a motorized starting gate. Here's how it's done. The horses line up behind a hinged gate mounted on a motor vehicle. As the vehicle begins to move to the starting line, the horses initiate their moving start, staying behind the gate. At the starting line, the wings of the gate are folded up, and the vehicle accelerates away from the horses.

The Winner Is a *"Beamer"*?

(Well, in a sense...) How is the winner of a race determined today? Why, with the best of technology, of course. A beam of light now spans the finish line: the horse with the nose that breaks the beam first is declared the winner.

Hot To Trot (Or *Not?*)

"As if conscious of his narrow escape from oblivion", said Hervey, "Peter The Great then began to improve."[62] According to the *Kalamazoo Gazette*, as a two-year old Peter was sometimes worked by Johnston at Browne's half-mile track on West Main, and trained at a racetrack near Grand Rapids.[63] At the beginning of August, Peter The Great clocked a mile in 2:27, a very nice time, and his training was eased up for a bit. Unfortunately, however, Peter took ill at that time, and was not able to be harnessed for a month. (Speaking of "harnessed", let's make sure you're mentally on the right track. If you've been picturing Peter being worked on the track with his trainer on his back, remember that Peter is a *trotter*, a horse that races pulling a sulky; he trains that way, he races that way.) Because of his sire's reputation for fast colt trotters, Peter had been entered in advance in many of the futurities; but, due to his slow training and to being sick, Streeter had to forfeit all of the less important races that would have given the horse at least *some* experience.[64] When Peter The Great recovered from his illness, he again had to relearn a lot that he had been taught—but this time, he did so more quickly than before.

Right Out of The Frying Pan Into The Fire...

The heat of late summer had given way to the cooler days of autumn by the time Peter The Great was ready. Only one race was left: the prestigious Junior Kentucky Futurity, the most important race in the nation for two-year olds, to be held in early October of 1897. Peter The Great was still carrying twenty ounces on his front feet, which gave the colt a "tendency to train sore".[65] (The weight was reduced later on, but Peter always wore heavy shoes to keep him in balance.) When the time came to ship Peter The Great to Lexington for the big race, he was looking pretty good: hard training had shaved Peter's best time down to 2:24¾.[66] Streeter wanted Peter The Great to start in the race; Johnston thought he was ready. And so it was that Peter—in what would be the first official race of his life—jumped right out of the frying pan and into the fire, pitted against colts and fillies that had been racing all season long.

"Watch Me Pull a Rabbit Out of My Hat!"

Well, not a rabbit out of a hat actually—what really got pulled out was more like a white handkerchief or a white flag. (Sometimes, too, a bell was rung.) And this was, of course, the way a horse race started in the old days. Before we're off to the races with Peter The Great, let's take a look how a harness race begins—the facts might surprise you. Unlike a Thoroughbred race (which starts from a complete standstill) trotting races began then—and they still do—from a *moving start*. When the racing official, on the inside of racetrack, ordered the trainers to line up, the drivers settled solidly into the seat of the sulky and moved the horses to line up at a spot about three-eighths of a mile before the starting line. At the signal, the horses moved towards the starting line, gaining speed; the race officially began at the starting line (which, on an oval track, is of course also the finish line at the end of the race).

The Amazing Race (Horse)

By the time the horses actually reach the starting line, they have worked up a lot of speed; in today's races, they'd be moving at something like 30–40 miles per hour, according to the Indiana Standardbred Hall of Fame. (Roughly speaking, a horse that races a one–mile course in a time of 2:00 would be racing at a speed of 30 miles per hour; a time of 1:55 would be at 40 miles per hour. Today, either time would be fairly standard, but that was *not* the case in Peter The Great's time: he had just clocked a mile in 2:24¾, as you'll recall.) So, if you think that racehorses move amazingly fast, you are absolutely correct. When the moving horses have achieved the starting line, the flag is dropped, and *that* is when the race begins.

"Ready Or Not, Here We Come"

The first Kentucky Futurity had been held in Lexington four years earlier at "The Red Mile", a course named for its track of red clay. It was early October of 1897 when Peter The Great was led off the train in Lexington, and entered a world completely unlike anything he had ever known. The town was teeming with people, all there for the fall Grand Circuit meets. Excitement was building as owners and spectators alike prepared for the big $10,000 race.[67] (That would be a purse of over $220,000 to us now.) And it was there, with no previous experience whatsoever on the racing circuit, that Johnston maneuvered Peter into position with the other six sulkies, the tension running high, the horses all snorting and blowing, tossing their heads. Peter The Great's chance of performing well in the first official race of his life, against other horses that had been racing steadily, looked dim— and Streeter and Johnston knew it. "The 1897 two–year–old crop was a vintage one", writes Hervey, "a fast and well–seasoned field". Hervey next comment went straight to the point. "Did it not savor almost of insanity to send to the post in such company a colt that had never before" even been in an official race? The favorite was a filly named Janie T. that Hervey says had been virtually unbeatable all that year, and he states plainly that she was "looking a certainty" to take the meet.[68]

Come A Little Bit Closer:
(You're My Kind of Horse; So Fast And ...)

It was time. The starter gave the signal for the moving start to begin, and the horses set off, muscles straining as they began gathering speed. The starting line was achieved, a flash of white—and the race had begun. There were two heats in the race that day, says Hervey. With Johnston in the seat of the sulky, Peter The Great brought in times of 2:17½ and 2:15¼, the time in the second heat beating his best training time by an amazing nine seconds. Peter The Great had been so close on the filly's heels that he helped spur her on to set a new world's record for two–year olds. And Peter's time was excellent—only a couple of seconds behind hers.[69]

"Riding the Rail" in Horse Racing

Does it make a difference where the horse is positioned in the race? Sure it does. The horse on the inside lane, the horse "riding the rail", actually has the shortest distance to travel. (Picture an oval track in your mind, with grass in the middle, and you'll be able to "see" that there is more distance for the horse to cover on the "outside" position.) The horse that rides the rail (actually, it's about three feet out from the rail, for safety) has the prime spot, the best on the field.

Rules of Engagement

How are the positions in a harness horse race determined? Generally speaking, positions in the first heat are assigned by judges—often assisted by horsemen—who randomly draw a position number, which is then paired with a horse's entry form, also drawn at random. After the first heat has been run, post positions are often earned by the order in which the horse finished in that heat, with the top finisher riding the rail, second–place next, and so on to the outside position.

"He Came Out of Nowhere To Be a Contender"

Peter The Great came in second in the race that day. And although things were never "rocky" for this unknown horse, (as they were for the unknown contender in the classic movie of that name), he certainly had gone the distance with the filly. And, as with the unknown in the movie, Peter The Great's first appearance made quite a stir. After having been sick and then missing training for a while, Peter had done unexpectedly well: in his first competition, the colt from Kalamazoo had beaten some top two-year olds, beating all but the winner with ease. The "something like twenty ounces" (of total weight) that Peter wore in front resulted in "gorgeous front action", with a step "so high and bold" it required elbow boots for his protection.[70] In a field of seven starters, he had taken second place in both heats, giving him second overall in the most famous race for two-year olds in the nation. Peter's success, astonishing for a colt that had never started in a race, was considered a triumph for Johnston, who had long been respected for his abilities. Accolades filled the trotting press, Hervey relates, praising the trainer's patience, his resourcefulness, and his refusal to give up on the colt.

Say It Isn't So...

With the excitement of the race behind them, Streeter took Peter The Great back to The Oaklands to winter in the snows of Michigan, looking towards his campaign as a three-year old. Eventually the snows receded, and the trees at The Oaklands began to bud: spring arrived in Kalamazoo. Johnston started Peter The Great back in training, and found that yet *again* he appeared to have forgotten all he'd learned. Instead of improving on the superb form he had shown in Lexington in the Futurity, he'd gone back to his earlier behavior. It took so long for Johnston to correct Peter The Great's poor form that, as before, the horse could not be entered in any of the early races Streeter and Johnston had been planning towards. His only start as a three-year old would, once again, bring him up against the best—this time, in the Senior Division of the Kentucky Futurity.

Things Are Really Starting To *Heat* Up

No, we're not talking about the weather here, not with fall just around the corner. It's actually *racing* heats we need to look at for a moment (with information provided by the U. S. Trotting Association) so you'll understand them when we get to Lexington for the next Futurity.[71] Unlike modern harness racing, where most races are conducted in a single dash, horses during the days of Peter The Great were expected to race more than once a day. Most races were made up of several "heats", or one-mile races, which gave every horse a chance to win. Heats varied in number and type from race to race, and from track to track. The stamina needed to race that often in a single day was certainly a testament to the Standardbreds of the era. Here's a bit of information that might help you get the idea:

~ ~ ~

Depending on the requirements of a specific race, many Standardbreds of Peter's time would race three, four, or sometimes even more heats in a single day. The overall race winner wasn't determined until a horse had *won* a specified number of heats—usually two or three. With the number of horses entered in a given race sometimes reaching into the double digits, it's easy to see how races might occasionally go for seven or eight heats if the field was evenly matched. (By the way, the only "winner" in a race is the one who crosses the finish line first; the others are said to "take second" or "take third".) Now that you've got that concept buckled down, it's time to head for the train.

Wild Horses Couldn't Keep Us Away (From The Race, That Is)

And so, as the leaves on the maple trees turned from greens to hues of orange, racing devotees once again made their annual pilgrimage to The Red Mile track at Lexington. This time, Peter was racing in the Senior Division of the Kentucky Futurity, the nation's most important race for three-year olds at the time. And again he found himself facing colts and fillies that were seasoned and fit, sharpened by a summer of campaigning. Peter The Great would make his first—and only—start as a three-year old, in a field of six, against the pick of the country, at the height of their form. Peter The Great was by now in good condition as well.

"One For The Money..."
The date was October 6: the year, 1898. It was "Senior day at the Trots", and the $10,000 purse was high; $7,300 of it (that translates to over $160,000 now) would go to the winner. The bet on the race's favorite was set at $35; Peter The Great brought $15. The track was soft from the rain of the previous day, but it wasn't a problem for the colt. The driver was Peter V. Johnston, who was more than ready—as was Peter—as they took the field with the other five horses. Trotting historian John Hervey was there in Lexington on the day of the race, and we hear the story in his words, as well as the words of R. A. Patton of the *Kalamazoo Gazette*.[72] Hervey tells us that for those who had expressed doubts about Peter The Great's abilities, "any uncertainty about the outcome...was speedily dispelled".[73] The *Gazette* phrases it well, telling us that "at the start of the first heat Peter The Great hit his stride, fought for the lead, took it"— and kept it, to which Hervey adds an equally descriptive "dashing home in 2:15¾".

"Two For The Show..."
When it was time for the next heat, the horses lined up, ready for the signal to start. Again the fine words Patton wrote in the *Gazette* describe Peter's performance in the race: "Scoring for the second heat, his great head held high, he handled as easy as on a practice spin on Browne's track. The field pounded to the starting line and there Peter The Great's matchless form as a trotter was his salvation. He hit stride again...swung into the lead and finished in front without a touch of the whip. Johnston's driving that day...was a thing of beauty and the way [Peter] swept away all opposition something never to forget."[74] Hervey says that Peter took that heat "still easier at the wire", with a time even better than that of the first heat: he had trimmed it to 2:14¼. (The crowd in the stands must have been rethinking their wagers by then...)

"Three To Get Ready..."
The sulkies lined up again, this time for the third, and final, heat. The excitement of the crowd was high, but even so, they were not expecting what they saw at the race that day. The horses moved into position, waiting for the sign; then moving at a trot, gaining momentum. The starter's signal was given, and—*they're off!* The noise in the stands was deafening, the excitement of the crowd building as the horses' hooves pounded the track, damp red clay flying. Johnston took the horse to the front, Peter The Great's powerful muscles straining to pull farther—and farther—and yet *farther* ahead, Johnston "allow[ing] him to sail so far away from the others that he appeared bent upon shutting them all out". Peter was so far ahead, Hervey states, that Johnston modified his speed a bit, easing him in the stretch, "despite which" he won by an amazing *twenty lengths!* Peter The Great set a new world's record with the win, taking the race with a time of 2:12½.[75]

You Do The Math...
Peter The Great won the Kentucky Futurity by twenty lengths that day; is that such a big deal? *You bet it is!* Let's stop for a second and see why the spectators went wild when Peter crossed the finish line twenty lengths ahead of the nearest horse. The distance by which a horse wins a race is measured in "lengths" of 10 feet (which is an average horse's length from the tip of its nose to its tail, when the horse is standing still).[76] Peter The Great won the three-year old Kentucky Futurity by twenty lengths (20 x 10 feet) or about 200 feet, so it's no wonder that he broke the world's record! (To give you an idea of the distance, Peter would have been ahead of the closest horse by a length roughly equal to *seven school buses parked end to end*.)

"...And 'Four' To Go!"
The Indiana Standardbred Hall of Fame tells us that when in full stride (meaning the distance of one complete stride, measuring from where a foot hits the ground to where that same foot hits the ground again, or one complete rotation) a racehorse can cover an extraordinary amount of distance—about 25 feet, in fact. During the final quarter of a mile race, trotting horses usually accelerate, making the finish exciting, extremely close, and spectacular to view. Imagine the thrill that day, watching from the stands, as Peter, with his long stride, hooves pounding the turf, crossed the finish line far ahead of the closest horse. And now, back to the track!

31

Some Day Your Prince Will Come...(Come In *First*, That Is...)
Peter The Great's first place win in the Kentucky Futurity created a great sensation, as Hervey recounts wonderfully for us here. "The ease" with which Peter took the heats..."the perfect manners displayed by the winner...the gallantry that distinguished him—his high head, slashing action, bold and spirited self-confidence—all combined to excite a wave of admiration tinged with that feeling of wonder when a horse...coming from nowhere carries off a great fixed event in all-conquering style." Writing years later, Hervey said that he "still vividly recalls the surge of exhilaration that prevailed" as Peter's fifty-seven year old driver, 'Peter V', was "obliged again and again to doff his cap and reveal his white [hair] in response to the applause as he and [Peter The Great] came jogging back to receive the roses and the silver trophy they had so superbly won".[77]

Peter The Great with trainer Johnston;
Kentucky Futurity, 1897 or 1898
(Courtesy, Western Michigan University Archives and Regional History Collections)

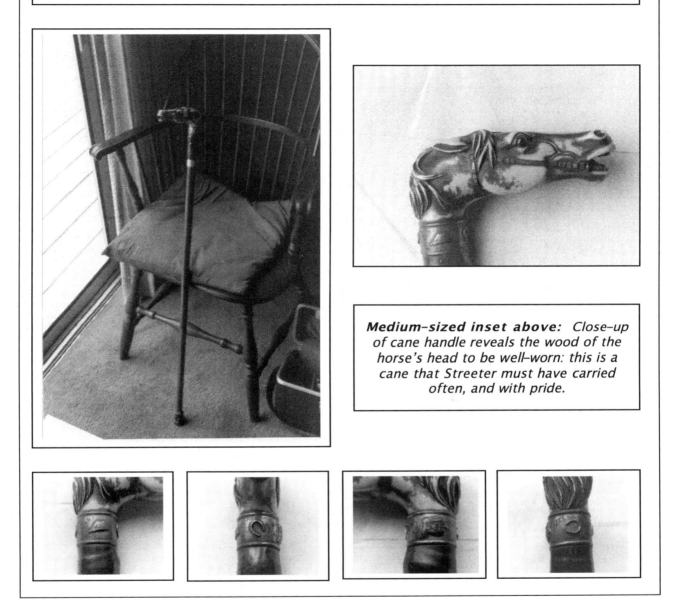

Daniel D. Streeter's cane, leaning against chair, commemorates Peter The Great's world-record breaking 1898 Kentucky Futurity win. (Courtesy, Western Michigan University Archives and Regional History Collections)

Medium-sized inset above: Close-up of cane handle reveals the wood of the horse's head to be well-worn: this is a cane that Streeter must have carried often, and with pride.

Smaller images, left to right: *First photo provides a close view of a trainer's cap on the right side of the cane. Shown next is the part of the cane just below the horse's chin; it records the name of the race "Kentucky Futurity" (above a horseshoe) with the year "1898" just below. Third shot, left side of the cane, presents an English saddle (shown sideways), a symbol denoting aristocracy. Last image offers the back of the cane, with a horse's flowing wooden mane above a horseshoe that has a "3" (the race was for three-year olds) set in its curve; beside that is a small "c", which indicates "colt". Carved above the horseshoe are the words:*
~Peter The Great~

Don't You Love It When a Plan Comes Together?

"The telegraph wires had no more than heralded" the news of the sensational performance of Peter The Great, relates Hervey with justifiable pride, "than [Peter] became the subject of vast discussion and much...comment and theorizing."[78] Newspapers were filled with stories about the virtually unknown three-year old colt from Kalamazoo. Peter The Great, forgotten by most since the Futurity the year before, now became famous both here and in Europe for winning all three heats of the Kentucky Futurity, and for doing it with relative ease. After the victory, Peter was again taken north by train to spend the winter in Michigan. Hervey said that when Peter arrived in Kalamazoo he "received the reception due a conquering hero", and his enthusiastic followers envisioned a great racing career ahead for the colt. The Oaklands must have been filled with visitors, the mansion aglow with lights on the first evening of their return, as the Streeter's friends flocked to see Peter The Great and join in the celebrations.

Praises for Peter

An article in the U.S. Trotting Association's *Hoof Beats* (written in 1995 by turf writer Dean A. Hoffman in celebration of the centennial of Peter's birth) said that "praises for Peter The Great fairly leapt off the pages" of *The Horse Review* following the Kentucky Futurity. "Not only did he out-trot, but also out-looked all his rivals. He is a bright cherry bay, finely molded from nose to tail, and one of the boldest going ones imaginable. He never lowered his head at any time, but carried it like a high-school horse," reported the sport's foremost journal of the time. Peter's Futurity win had caught the attention of many trotting horse fanciers. And, says Hoffman, on the train leaving Lexington after the race, Streeter reportedly met one of them—a Boston millionaire by the name of J. Malcolm Forbes.[79]

Let's Make a Deal

Although he had seen Peter The Great only once—during the race—Forbes had been so taken with Peter's performance that he wanted to buy the horse. It must have been a difficult proposition for Daniel Streeter to consider, coming as it did on the heels of the big win. The deciding factor must surely have been that Peter's trainer, Johnston, had notified Streeter that he wanted to retire from the rigors of racing and "devote himself to lighter duties" as manager of the Streeter farm.[80] Unable to find another man he thought was capable of training Peter as he required and deserved, Streeter would before long agree to Forbes' offer. The total worth of the deal was about $20,000, a combination of $15,000 in cash (that cash would be worth well over $300,000 today) plus conditions that included Streeter getting breeding service for ten of his mares from Peter The Great, or from any of Forbes' other sires.[81]

Into Every Life A Little Rain Must Fall

The new year had hardly begun when Kalamazooans picked up their morning papers and found to their dismay that Peter The Great would be leaving them. The time came all too soon. Initially, the trip to Forbes Farm in Canton, Massachusetts (not far from Boston) must have seemed to Peter like the other trips he had taken; he had traveled across long distances twice before, from Michigan to Kentucky—and back. From this trip he would not return. He would never again roam the paddock at The Oaklands in Kalamazoo, never again see his owner Daniel Streeter, never again work with Johnston, who had been Peter's sole trainer. (Johnston would remain in Kalamazoo until his sudden death over a dozen years later, in May of 1912.)[82] And Peter would miss the familiar faces of many other people he had known during the years as he grew to maturity in Kalamazoo. The sun had set on his old life; a new day was dawning. Peter The Great would find his new life filled with a few bits of sunshine that came and went like quicksilver—and find it filled with many stormy days, as well.

Burning The Candle at Both Ends...

Peter The Great left the snow and cold of Michigan behind in late January of 1899, arriving at Forbes Farm in New England—where it was probably at least as cold—on the first day of February. Shortly after Peter's arrival, Forbes announced that Peter The Great "would make a limited stud season at a fee of $2,500", an amount as "unprecedented" as Forbes' $20,000 purchase price had been and "one never since demanded for a trotting sire", to quote Hervey in an article he wrote about Peter in 1947, nearly half a century later.[83] (Unprecedented it certainly was: that stud fee would be like asking for roughly $55,000 today; at that price, Peter The Great probably didn't draw many—*any?*— mares from outside the farm.) As was common practice in that era, Forbes stood Peter The Great at stud during that spring and early summer serving a select group of mares, simultaneously training him for his four-year old campaign.[84] Serious training for the fall Grand Circuit competition would begin after the stud season had ended. "Burning the candle at both ends" in this fashion was, Hervey reveals, a procedure that many in racing considered to be "essentially mistaken and genetically improper and unwise".[85]

Peter The Great Continued To Pipe a Peck of People...

Often, during the years following Peter The Great's big Futurity win, horsemen passing through Kalamazoo would pay a visit to the Streeter farm where the winner of the 1898 Kentucky Futurity had been born. Although he no longer owned Peter The Great, Daniel Streeter—and all Kalamazooans—were able to talk about "their" colt when the Grand Circuit races came to town for one week each summer. "Every Grand Circuit meet saw [visiting horsemen] trooping to the stable", wrote R. A. Patton in a *Kalamazoo Gazette* article.[86] There they would head to Peter's stable and stand in reverent awe before the stall where Peter The Great had been foaled. Streeter enjoyed the visitors, and was always willing to regale them with stories about the colt and his life in Kalamazoo.

Frame barn at The Oaklands in Kalamazoo was the home of Peter The Great.
(Used with the permission of the KALAMAZOO GAZETTE)

It is believed (according to a caption in a Western Michigan University pamphlet about
The Oaklands) that Peter The Great was foaled in the northwest corner on the lower level of
this frame barn, which once stood near the current site of the garage for The Oaklands.
Horses were brought up in the barn elevator from the lower level to the first floor.
There they were hitched to surreys and then brought around to the east side
of the mansion, where the ladies came out (under a sheltering canopy)
when they wanted to be driven to town.[87]

"Let's Get It On"

Let's pull up for a minute, settle back, and take a look into the wardrobe of Peter The Great. (No lions or witches in *this* wardrobe, though, contrary to what a boy named Peter encounters in a wardrobe in a different story.) The focus of *our* story is a horse, and his wardrobe was the kind that is worn. And it was certainly full: when Peter took his record as a four-year old in New York later on, he was wearing nine-ounce iron shoes with three-ounce weights in front, and five-ounce shoes behind. And Hervey said he wore *four different kinds* of boots.

~ ~ ~

The first were elbow boots (a leather piece or cup, rather like an elbow-pad for a human) that protected his elbows from being struck when he was in stride. (He had to wear these because of the bold, high stepping action of his front feet.) Next were close-fitting quarter-boots; the third were shin-and-ankle boots, worn forward, (meaning on his front legs); and the last, worn on his hind legs, were a pair of combination ankle and cuff boots, in addition to five-ounce shoes. (It must really have taken some time and patience on the part of both horse and trainer to get all of *that* on.)

There Was a *Need* For *Speed*

Peter The Great had passed out of the hands of Johnston, the leading trainer and driver in Michigan at the time, and into the hands of a young New Englander named Henry Titer, causing "many heads to be shaken" by horsemen in Kalamazoo and around the nation, reports Hervey. Johnston had been a "holdover from the past" and had "trained [Peter] upon principles only slightly modified from those of forty years before". Johnston's system of speed development had been completely opposite to that of Peter The Great's new trainer, a young man who had come up almost "overnight" and had quickly climbed to be highly placed in his profession. Titer was of the new school that wanted "speed, speed, and still again more speed", Hervey says. Peter was rushed into training with "almost no intermission from the moment real track work began"—and he did not respond to the change well.[88]

"Get Off My Back"

Not surprisingly, this "abrupt change soon began to develop disturbing results", states Hervey. Titer found he had difficulties in "getting [Peter] balanced [and] keeping him so", which was complicated by Peter's "tendency to train sore...probably a hangover from his training" by Johnston, who "in order to do with him what he had, was obliged to be severe".[89] Peter The Great had been carrying roughly twenty ounces of weight on his front feet as two-year at Lexington (as mentioned before), and "while this was lightened up somewhat later", Hervey explains, "it was never possible to balance him except with plenty of iron".[90] According to turf writer Ken McCarr in an article in *Harness Horse Magazine*, the least Peter ever wore was nine ounces in front, with three-ounce toe weights.[91] Wearing the weights may have seemed reminiscent of the old days in Kalamazoo, but Peter must have been quite aware that his life with his new owner and new trainer was very different from what it had been before his sale to Forbes. "It is doubtful if any colt with a racing experience of only two starts, spaced a year apart, ever had more done with him or was kept at it more rigorously than was [Peter]", according to Hervey.[92] Peter The Great must have heartily wished that everyone would just "get off his back" and let him have some peace for a while.

Grand Illusions

One of Forbes' greatest desires had been to enter Peter The Great, the horse that had taken the Futurity by twenty lengths, in the home Grand Circuit meeting to be held at nearby Readsville. This was the $10,000 Massachusetts Stake, and Forbes hoped for a likewise spectacular win. Training went slowly, however, and Forbes "became impatient", as Hervey puts it, as the weeks slipped by.[93] It soon became obvious that Peter The Great would not be ready in time for the meet, and Forbes grand hopes "had to be abandoned".

36

"So Now You're Back..."

The end of summer was at hand by the time Peter The Great was ready. Forbes took the horse to Hartford, Connecticut for the Charter Oak Stake, to be held on August 29, 1899. "Those who had been watching Peter" in his training, said Hervey, reported him as "clothed with speed but a somewhat doubtful quantity" for the race. Just Peter's third start in as many years, it was also his four-year old debut—and his first race with Henry Titer holding the reins. They took the track, lined up against the favorite, Charley Herr, and nine other horses. Titer started with an "easy opening" heat; Peter took second place to Charley Herr. After that, the trainer "cut [Peter] loose" in the next three heats, and "he closed out the race as he willed", with times of 2:08¾, 2:09¼, and 2:09½.[94] Peter The Great won the $3,225 (a sum worth more than $70,000 in today's money) "early closer" meet that day, taking home the winner's share of the purse for his new owner. "Peter The Great is once more Peter The *Great!*" raved the critics, and interest in the $5,000 feature event to be trotted in New York the following week escalated considerably.

Tune In Next Week...

The lazy days of summer were over—especially for horse racing fans, since the fall season, with its race after race, was now commencing. Just one week later Titer and Peter The Great were off to Yonkers, New York, for the inaugural meeting, the very first race, at the new Empire City Track, held on September 4, 1899.[95] It was Peter The Great's second race as a four-year old, and this time he was breaking precedent: instead of one *year* between races, he had just one *week*--and this with a trainer that he was not yet very accustomed to. Would Peter The Great once again forget what he knew? Might he have given his all in the previous race, and have nothing left? Tune in next week...

"Any Given Sunday"

Regardless of what day of the week it is, you never really know what can happen in any sporting contest. Stakes for the inaugural race were high, set at $5,000, recounts Hervey, (more than $110,000 now). Peter The Great took the field with eleven other spirited colts and fillies, all ready as could be. Despite the decisive victory the previous week, Peter was still not a shoe-in for winning the race. He was indeed looking good—yet there were still those other times, the ones that kept his owner and trainer a bit "off balance" themselves, in regards to Peter's chances. Titer focused on thinking the best as they waited, lined up with the others for the first heat, the drivers' clothes flashing bright patterns in the sun. Moving now—the signal—*go!* And with the signal, Titer went right to it, "full of confidence", and "gave Peter his head". He "rushed down to the half [mile] in 1:02¾, which took all the wind out of the sails of the pursuit", wrote Hervey. Peter The Great took the first heat with a time of 2:07¼—his lifetime best. But the race wasn't over; the final heat saw him "in front all the way and romping home" in 2:08¼.[96] It had been an easy victory—and it was his third win in a row.

Go Straight To The Horse's Mouth...

Just a bit more on equipment, before we take off again to the races. Horses are fitted with a *bit* (a metal bar attached to a bridle) which rests in the horse's mouth; the driver uses this and the bridle to guide and control the direction of the horse.

...*Then To His Eyes*

Horses have eyes that are set towards the side of their heads, which gives them a wide range of vision. For racing, Peter The Great was fitted with a "*blind*" bridle, a type that focuses the horse's vision straight ahead, (effectively eliminating sight of movements to the side that might startle the horse). Now that we've completed our peek into Peter's wardrobe, we're off to experience more of the magic of horse racing. And for that we don't need our imaginations: once again, we have the real story, as narrated by John Hervey.

"I'm The King of The World!"
With a thrill reminiscent of a scene in a recent movie blockbuster of titanic proportions, and "following so closely upon his Hartford triumph", said Hervey, "this new victory placed [Peter The Great] on a pinnacle". The colt that had been foaled in Kalamazoo was now at the top of his world, and those writing about him knew it. "He can beat any other trotter in training" ran one of the articles…"He can beat the stallion record", said another. "He can beat the world's record [for four-year olds] when he gets to Lexington if they try with him", declared a third.[97]

"Play It Again, Sam"
Forbes must have savored the triumph of the win in New York, and its resultant publicity; perhaps it even atoned somewhat for the difficulties the horse had given him. Peter The Great now had three weeks off, in preparation for his closing races in Louisville and Lexington. The time passed quickly; before long, Massachusetts was left behind as Titer and Peter headed for Kentucky. The race at Louisville with a field of just seven entries (including Charlie Herr, whom he had beaten nearly a month before) was held on September 26, 1899. The stakes were again $5,000; the driver, Henry Titer. For this race the confident atmosphere had altered, comments Hervey, as some said Peter The Great "had been nodding" in his recent training. "They may beat him today" went the rumors before the race, and "he's not the same colt we saw at New York". But at the end of the race, Peter had shaken off the favorite decisively; his times were 2:11 and 2:10.[98] Peter The Great's winning streak now stood at four in a row. Then off again to another race, still in Kentucky, but back in Lexington, the city of his big Futurity triumph.

I'll Betcha He'll Win
The Transylvania, a stake for "all" ages of racehorses, was held one week later, on October 5. Once again, John Hervey narrates for us.[99] "It was a hectic and tumultuous session of the 'Trots'", he declares. Contributing to the overall excitement was the presence of Thomas W. Lawson "whose betting operations kept the headlines aflame the length and breadth of the land". Lawson's money, it was said, was "set in" on Peter The Great. At the opening of the race, odds were on Peter, who was the favorite at $100; bets on the field ran $30 to $40. (For those who follow horse racing, the betting system used in the 1800's, according to a racing expert, would have been different from the pari-mutuel wagering system in place today; it was a rather complex type of "auction" system—we won't even try to explain it here.) No matter how you figure it, it's plain to see that the crowd was backing Peter The Great that autumn day.

And They're Off!
The "grand field" of nine horses was ready, and Hervey tells us the entire story in his own inimitable fashion.[100] A vintage photograph (not shown here) of the first heat shows that Charley Herr (#7) whom Peter had already beaten twice, had drawn the inside position, riding the rail; Peter The Great (#3) had drawn the fifth position. The horses started off, the flag was dropped, and once more the horses' hooves were pounding around the track. "Titer stepped his colt right to the front, led all the way, and won sitting still by open daylight in 2:09¼", with Charley Herr crossing the finishing line next. The win in the first heat gave Peter The Great the coveted inside position on the track for the second heat, as can be seen by a close look at the position board in the race photo on the next page. (If you have sharp eyes or a magnifying glass, that is.) The posted numbers of the horses show Peter The Great now riding the rail, with Charley Herr in the second position. The second heat went much the same way as the first, with Peter The Great again the winner, followed by Charley Herr—and Peter had trimmed his time to 2:08¼.

Peter The Great winning the second heat of the Transylvania, with Charley Herr behind him; October 5, 1899, in Lexington, Kentucky.
(Courtesy, U. S. Trotting Association)

The Neighs (Don't) Have It

Prior to the third heat, Hervey details, Peter was the "favorite at five to one over the field" in the betting. The third heat began. At the three-quarter mile mark, Peter was again out in front, with "two contenders hanging on grimly", and Peter The Great "seeming to hold them at bay. After straightening out for home, he began to draw away and the race looked over, but suddenly...he left his stride, [and] the other pair swept by". Although many of his supporters must have said *nay*—it couldn't have happened—Peter The Great took third in the third heat.

He Who Hesitates Is Lost

The agitation that resulted was "indescribable". Two different explanations of what had occurred were "heatedly put forth", according to Hervey. One group maintained that the cause of the break in Peter's stride "was his driver's turning in his sulky to look around, which threw the colt off balance". The other faction denied this, arguing that Peter "was weakening so fast that Titer felt obliged to take stock of the competition in an effort to stave off disaster". Before the fourth heat, Peter The Great had dropped from $100 down to $50 in the pools.

39

We Need More (Horse) Power?
The fourth heat began, Titer moving Peter The Great "to the lead in a flash". Peter "assumed a commanding lead and at the home turn his backers began cheering". But now a horse "hitherto unsteady and out of the fight, came [on] with a wet sail", according to Hervey. "Just inside the distance Peter The Great repeated his break of the previous heat", and began to draw away. "When [the other horse] nailed him", Peter made another break "and ran under the wire, apparently a nose victor"—but the verdict went to the other stallion, leaving Peter The Great in second. "Again harsh criticism was leveled at Titer", Hervey states. The fifth heat now. Titer "sent [Peter] out to make the pace. He led into the stretch, but this time broke at the seven-eights" mile mark, finishing the heat in fifth place. Only heat winners started in the sixth and seventh heats; Peter finished a "very tired third" in both. Overall in the race, Peter The Great took third place—the only time he would take that position in his entire racing career.[101]

The War of the Words
The "warfare of words" about the race, both "spoken and written", reports Hervey, was "bitter and sustained". Titer was severely condemned by those who maintained that the defeat was not Peter The Great's fault. Others said "as long as he [Peter] can have the track to himself and nothing bothers him, he looks like a world–beater. But once [the other horses] take him to town, it's another story".[102] Peter The Great's supporters were outraged. And Forbes couldn't have been happy with his horse's performance in the race. Fortunately, although Peter was the main topic of interest for the writers, he wasn't the *only* one. It seemed that, before the sixth heat, Thomas Lawson "with a last flamboyant gesture" had "laid $5,000 against $10,000", betting that Peter The Great would win the heat. Lawson had gambled his money—and lost. Hervey concluded, "It [was] computed that the defeat of Peter The Great had cost [Lawson] over $30,000".[103] (No wonder they talked about Lawson's losses; today, that loss would be more than $660,000.)

This Race Was Peter's *"007"*
Top secret? On the contrary, the seventh race in Peter The Great's career was anything but. On Monday, the second week of the 'Trots', the "excitement was little less than [it had been] on Transylvania day", which Hervey maintains had been high indeed. The $3,000 (similar to over $60,000 today) Ashland Stake in Lexington, held around the twelfth of October, would be raced on a track that was soft and therefore tiring, due to heavy rains the day before. The odds "showed the kind of race that was expected": before the race began, Peter The Great was the betting favorite at $225, followed closely by a fine stallion named Tommy Britton at $200. (The rest of the bets were at $50 and $20.) Peter and the other stallion "so far outclassed their opponents that no way could be figured for [any other horse] to win, unless", Hervey says, "they killed each other off in speed duels in the opening heats". Which, he states, is precisely what happened.[104]

Bring It On
The signal was given, and the horses were off. "There they goooooo!" was the cry that rang in the ears of the crowd. Both stallions were noted "front runners", Hervey relates, and "they began their test for the supremacy at the word in the first heat".[105] Hervey describes the excitement: "they sped to the first quarter in flat :32", a speed which was "dizzy[ing] considering that they were obliged, on account of the soft going, to keep out three sulky widths" from the rail. "Once straight in the back stretch, the clip increased to one never before witnessed in a trotting race as they covered the second quarter in :29½, this being the first time that one was ever officially timed in :30 or better." At the half, the other stallion, "on the inside, showed a neck ahead...around the upper turn Titer called on Peter The Great, but he was unable to gain an inch, though maintaining his position as they swung for home". The effect the rapid pace was having on the horses was beginning to show. At the finish line for the first heat, Peter The Great came in second, just half a length behind the stallion.

Hotter Than...Heck
"Both stallions were much distressed", Hervey notes, "for the day was close and sultry."[106] The humidity was unbearable, the sun beating down unmercifully on horses and drivers alike. In the stands it was the same. Men, clad in suits, removed hats frequently to apply handkerchiefs to foreheads wet with sweat. The women, corsets drawn so tight that breathing was hampered, were likewise stifling in dresses made of yards of material. And ladies' hats, considered an essential part of the fashions of the day, protected the complexion from the sun, but left the wearer warmer yet. Everyone wished heartily for the weather to change—but the only changes that afternoon were in the betting odds.

"I'm Tired, So Tired..."
Before the second heat, the odds changed greatly. Hervey tells us that Peter The Great, who had started the race the favorite at $225, had dropped to just $14; the stallion, down now from the original $200 to $50. When the second heat began, it "was another two–horse race", the stallions "racing lapped to the distance", Peter The Great winning "by about a length in 2:12¼". Both horses were now exhausted due to the weather, and a different horse entirely "took the next three heats with little effort". In the final heat Peter finished second, taking second overall in the race. Peter "had come to Lexington...considered a coming champion", Hervey wrote. "He left it with trailing colors."[107]

Is That Your Final Answer?
A "feeling of uncertainty" had been aroused regarding the horse, discloses Hervey, though many of Peter The Great's friends remained loyal. In an attempt to counter the uncertainty, "his admirers pointed out that [Peter] was a four year–old colt waging war against the best aged horses in training, and that before beginning his campaign he had been required to make a stud season". There were several other theories, as well as this one, to account for Peter The Great's failure to take first place in his past two races.[108] One theory went back to the "heroic methods" of Johnston to "get [Peter] to the Kentucky Futurity in such brilliant form without having previously raced him either season". Comments Hervey, "there is a strong probability" that those efforts, "while grandly successful at the time, later on exacted their price". Another theory was made up of several things: the "great difficulty" in straightening his gait, his "lay–ups and sick spells", the necessity of heavy weights to "perfect his gait", and the "rushing" that was done at the end of each stud season to get Peter into a race.[109] And, of course, there were also the different training styles of Johnston and Titer. In the end, perhaps the final answer might simply have been—all of these theories combined.

Diamonds And Dust...
Peter The Great's four–year old season was likened to "diamonds and dust" in an article by turf writer Dean Hoffman in USTA's *Hoof Beats*.[110] When Peter was good, he was brilliant; but when he was off–form, as he was at Lexington that autumn, his reputation lay trampled in the dust. Peter's supporters, Hervey details, claimed that the doubts about Peter "were unduly exaggerated" and that "with another season's maturity and different tactics he would restore himself" the following season.[111] The new century began with Peter The Great again spending a season in stud, serving mares in the spring of 1900. But, when Titer began training him for his five–year old campaign, "Peter's progress was not flattering", concedes Hervey. It was put forth that Peter The Great would be "given a long rest". He would not race at all in the 1900 season, so that he could emerge upon the Grand Circuit scene once again, a "giant refreshed", in 1901.[112]

For Whom The Bell Tolls...

But it was not to be. In 1901, Peter once again failed at training. Hervey announces that "Finis" was now written to Peter's racing career, writing with finality, and obvious regret, that "Peter The Great was never again to answer the starter's bell".[113] Peter had thrilled the racing world with his wins, and his prospects for the future had been bright; but no longer. As Dean A. Hoffman put it nearly a century later in his article *Reflections on the Centennial of Peter The Great's Birth*, "The toll had been extracted. Peter had nothing left to give".[114] The race on that stifling October day in Lexington, just before the turn of the century, had been Peter's last.

The Swan Song of Peter The Great

Although the Lexington race had been Peter The Great's swan song, the memory of his racing career still ripples in the waters of the harness racing world, for those familiar with his story. Peter The Great had started in just seven races. Of those races, reports Hervey, Peter had won four, taken two seconds and one third, and had taken a total of $17,050 in purses (the equivalent of over $375,000 now) for his two owners.[115] Peter The Great would race no more. From the first year of the twentieth century, and for many years thereafter, he would be used solely at stud.

The Thrill Is Gone...

The close of Peter The Great's racing career in what Hervey refers to as a "double fiasco" was "without doubt an intense disappointment" to Peter's owner.[116] New England millionaire Forbes, "who seldom left home to see his horses perform elsewhere and [who] was noted for his impassivity regarding them, both public and private", Hervey says, "had made the trip to Lexington with the expectation of being richly rewarded". Although Forbes gave no indication of it at the time, he "must have reacted inwardly if not outwardly to the course of events", says Hervey, writing "that we may trace back to...there his later attitude toward Peter The Great is psychologically probable". Hervey adds the following to that remark: "The germ of aversion for the colt was planted in [Forbes'] breast, and it only required further stimulus to produce visible results", a stimulus, declares Hervey, that "was provided the following winter when Mr. Forbes undertook to [race] the young horse on the Boston show path."[117]

Hey—What's With The *Sleigh?*

Hervey specifies that "complete control of both stride and speed in all spots" was necessary for racing on the Boston show path, which required a "whirlwind" tempo that Peter was "unable to meet". Besides control, the Boston show circuit required maneuverability in tight places, said Karen Greengard in an article in the *Michigan Harness Horseman*, skills that "were never the talents of the heavily booted and weighted horse".[118] Peter The Great's "complete failure" at this type of racing, as Hervey assessed it, further increased Forbes' dislike of the horse. Compounding the situation, explains historian Leon W. Miller in an article in the *W.M.U. Magazine*, was the custom of wealthy men of the day, who "owned fast horses and drove them for pleasure and sport...especially...on the snow paths in winter". Forbes attempted to use Peter The Great in this way, having him pull a cutter (a light sleigh).[119] But with his mixed and awkward gait, Peter was simply not suited for either the Boston show path *or* the winter snow path.

Pride and Prejudice

Miller relates a story (often written about but unconfirmed) that one day in winter, while pulling a cutter in public, Peter The Great slipped in the snow on a streetcar track and fell,[120] to Forbes utter mortification. While that particular story was not addressed by Hervey, his 1947 article did include the following statement, referring back to Peter's poor performance on the Boston show path: Forbes "had the discomfiture of being lost in the struggle instead of riding at [the] head". Hervey states that "after a series of such discomfitures—which unavoidably were conspicuous—we may credit as authentic the anecdote current at the time—that, dismounting from behind [Peter], Mr. Forbes tossed the reins to a waiting groom with the admonition: 'take that horse away and never bring him to me to drive again!'"[121] It was said that following this incident, Forbes, angry and humiliated, never did ask for Peter The Great again.

Cinderella Story

Once upon a time, there had been a young horse with a good owner, a fine trainer, and what must have been a fairly contented life at his home at The Oaklands in Kalamazoo. That pleasant life was gone now for good. According to Hervey, while Forbes continued "using [Peter The Great] to a limited degree as a sire", he now banished him, "took the extreme step of decreeing his removal from the stallion barn and [isolated him] in a remote stable, where he was kept incommunicado".[122] Forbes forbade the stablemen from showing Peter to the public, ordering that "unless they expressly desired it, he should not be shown to visitors nor in any way brought to their attention". Hervey tells us, in addition, that Peter The Great now "received only the most casual care".

"That's Outrageous..."

Peter The Great began to show the effects of the poor treatment. Hervey reveals that "those who insisted upon being allowed to see him" reported that Peter was "treated like an outcast"; he was "thin in flesh, his coat rough and unkempt, his deportment nervous and unhappy".[123] During the same time, according to Hervey, Forbes provided excellent care for two other sires to whom he was partial. Peter's circumstances at the farm summon thoughts of the fairy tale about a princess who was dressed in rags and was kept hidden from the world, while two others favored in the household received the best of everything. Peter The Great, who had been royalty himself for a brief but shining time, was in much the same position.

"Please Don't Let Me Be Misunderstood"

According to Hervey, there was talk that, as a result, Peter The Great had "become a 'stall walker' and [was] dangerous to handle". Why Forbes "kept on breeding to him under these circumstances adds to the complexity of the matter", Hervey observes, "but this he did, including even his best mare".[124] During the five seasons that Peter The Great stood at stud at Forbes Farm, he sired an impressive twenty-three record performers.[125] (*Record performers* are horses that have won official trotting or pacing races; make sure you get this concept down pat, as it is important later on in Peter's story.) Several of the mares mated with Peter had been sent from Daniel Streeter in Kalamazoo, as had been set out in the sales agreement between Streeter and Forbes. "Such was the situation in the spring of 1903", explains Hervey, when "the fortunes of Peter The Great had reached an almost incredibly low ebb as contrasted with his high tide of fame four seasons previous." Then Peter's daughter, Sadie Mac, appeared as if by magic on the racing scene: she herself became the key that opened Peter's door.

"And Then Along Came"...(No, Not Mary)...*Sadie Mac*

Although three-year old Peter had been mated, just once, in 1898 (during his last year on the Streeter farm in Kalamazoo), it was not until the following year, his first year with Forbes, that Peter The Great's stud service had begun in earnest, according to statistics provided by Hervey. In the 1899 season, at the age of four, Peter The Great had been mated with a number of mares at Forbes Farm, from which he got his first four foals.[126] One of those foals was Sadie Mac; born in 1900, she was the first of Peter The Great's foals to appear in public. Sadie Mac caused a sensation when she became the unbeaten three-year old champion of 1903, sweeping all of the Grand Circuit classics and finishing the season by taking the Kentucky Futurity. It was the first time that a previous Futurity winner had sired a foal that would *also* become a winner of that elite race.[127] Sadie Mac earned a total of $22,000 for her owner; her sale that autumn brought in an additional $20,000.[128] (Her owner would have taken in something over $425,000 with *each* of those figures in our day.) Sadie Mac created such a furor, said Hervey, that many in the trotting world began to say "what will Malcolm Forbes think of Peter The Great *now?*"

43

Part Four:
The Breeding Years

Sold at Old Glory Auction

Life with W. E. D. Stokes of Lexington

Sold to Stoughton Fletcher III of Indy

The 'king of sires' at Laurel Hall Farm

'Peter Went to Sleep'

"Just Turn Around, You're Not Welcome Any More..."
What he thought became almost immediately apparent, as Forbes took advantage of the headlines Sadie Mac had made to try to get rid of the stallion he no longer wanted. Peter The Great was consigned to the "Old Glory" auction at Madison Square Garden in New York, where horses were sent when their owners no longer wished to keep them. Hervey tells us that the two–week long Old Glory sale of 1903 had almost 1,050 horses.[129] Peter The Great was No. 740, and was on the slate for December 2; when the auction day arrived, his presence was met with interest—and uncertainty. When it was his turn, Peter The Great was led in and displayed to the audience, and was greeted by just a "scattering" of applause, Hervey writes. A "well–worded tribute" was delivered by the auctioneer, in which he "enlarged upon [Peter's] achievements first as a performer and then as a sire". It was time for the auction to begin.

"Do You Feel Lucky, Punk?"
Lucky? Not likely. *Punky?* Perhaps. When Peter The Great was led into the ring that day, the neglected horse was not in good condition. Hervey indicates that Peter was rather thin[130] but "presented a better appearance than many had expected in view of the rumors afloat", and he "showed few signs of nervousness".[131] Peter's left hock (which helps to support the horse's weight) was noticeably enlarged, likely caused by the physical strain of his stud activities. Forbes provided what could be politely termed an "interesting" owner's statement for the auction, writing that Peter The Great was "in condition for any use...has been driven regularly on the road this year since his stud season was over...is not afraid of electric cars, steam rollers, automobiles or anything that I know of".[132]

"Take a Chance On Me..."
The auctioneer called for bids upon Peter The Great, describing him, says Hervey, as "the most desirable young trotting stallion that [has] ever been sent into a sale ring". Uncertainty prevailed, as rumors of the state of the horse had been circulating. According to Hervey, "opening bids of $10,000 were asked for, with silence ensuing". The auctioneer dropped the figure gradually down to $5,000, and "still silence reigned". The bid then went lower. Only two men present at the auction seemed to have any real desire for the horse, and apparently neither wanted to go too high in the bidding. The first was Peter The Great's former owner, Daniel Streeter of Kalamazoo; the other, the former owner of Sadie Mac.[133]

The Price Is Right
"With great difficulty" the auctioneer managed to get the high bid "above $2,500", Hervey concedes. Then suddenly a new bidder entered the scene.[134] Peter Duryea of New York came forward, urged on by a sports writer, a great admirer of Peter The Great, who acted as an advisor in Duryea's selections. Duryea's closing bid of $5,000 proved decisive, relates Hervey. "Going once, going twice...*sold!*" the auctioneer shouted gratefully, with a firm rap of his gavel—and the deal was done. Surely being sold at auction would bring about a better situation for Peter The Great than the five years he had spent at Forbes Farm. Forbes, who had not attended the auction, arrived at the Garden later in the day. Upon being told the price obtained for Peter The Great in the proceedings, Forbes responded that it was "one of the best sales [the auctioneer] ever made". (Indeed it was: that transaction today would bring the seller over $100,000.)

"You Wouldn't Listen To Me"

According to Hervey, Duryea had a partner named W. E. D. Stokes. William Stokes, who had not attended the auction, was reportedly most displeased that his partner had paid $5,000 for the outcast stallion, and refused to listen when Duryea maintained that the purchase price would prove to be a good investment.[135] Quite a disagreement was said to have ensued between the two men; consequently, for a time, Duryea seriously considered sending Peter The Great, as his own "personal venture", to fill a stud position at the country manor Duryea owned in England. Hervey says that not long after the auction, however, Stokes was approached by "an agent of would-be American buyers with an offer of $8,000 for the stallion".[136] This offer apparently caused Stokes to reconsider (not surprising: that'd be an offer of $170,000 for us now) as he "later changed his mind and took over a half-interest" in Peter. (Later still, Stokes would reverse his earliest position, claiming that he had actually ordered the purchase.)[137]

Don't Even *Think* About It...

Hervey elaborates that for two months the destiny of Peter The Great "hung in the balance", effectively demonstrated by the fact that, although Peter was bought on the second day in December, Duryea did not announce the horse for service at his farm in Kentucky until the second week in February.[138] Hervey notes that ever after, when he wrote articles about Peter The Great, he always took great care to record the full details of Peter's sale at the auction, both "to provide authentic information" and also to show "how completely at the mercy of events the horse was, how easily [the events] might have been swayed in various directions and the entire course of breeding history thereby diverted into different channels".[139] The idea of the history of harness racing in America—without the enormous influence Peter The Great would provide as a sire—makes racing fans today shy away, shaking their heads at the thought.

Don't Look a Gift Horse In the Mouth

Peter was hardly a gift horse, (not with that $5,000 price tag), but a quick look in his or any horse's mouth can be quite revealing. While Hervey made no mention of the condition of Peter's teeth at the time of the auction, we'll point out some facts about neglected teeth here, (as they will add some bite to Peter's story). Broken or jagged teeth can cause pain and cuts to the tongue, keeping the horse from eating well, and contributing to a myriad of problems: poor coat, poor weight, poor athletic training and performance, a general lack of condition, colic—even behavioral problems. Once a horse's teeth have been filed smooth (which is called floating and should be done at least once a year), experts say it's amazing how quickly a horse will gain weight and generally improve. (Age, also, can also be determined by a look in a horse's mouth: first, to see if all of the permanent teeth are in, and second, by noting the straightness of the teeth. Horsemen know that the younger the horse is, the straighter the teeth; the older the horse, the more the teeth begin to protrude, eventually meeting in an angled point, and the more the gums begin to shrink back, making the teeth seem longer.) But getting back to Peter and the old adage we started with, we're admonished not to look too closely at something we've been given, but to be grateful for whatever comes our way—regardless of its condition.

"That's The Way...I Like It"

Uh huh. But not at first. Peter The Great was "looking bad" when he arrived at Patchen Wilkes Farm after his sale to Duryea, and Hervey reports that the horse was received in Lexington "with much curiosity and considerable doubt".[140] Hervey in fact says that Forbes' aversion for Peter The Great had "led to not only his neglect and mismanagement" at Forbes Farm, but to "something verging upon abuse".[141] At the time, according to Hervey, Peter The Great "weighed but 978 pounds, was in poor condition and ill tempered".[142] He responded rapidly to the expert care he received, however; he improved greatly in a short time and "his studbook was filled within a month".[143] Hervey reports that he often visited Peter The Great at the farm in Lexington after the sale, and found him "extremely docile and intelligent", and that "his manners were of the best".[144] One year after the auction, relates Hervey, Peter "weighed 1175 pounds and had become kind and pleasant...he remained thereafter of perfect disposition".[145]

Two, Four, Six, *Eight... Who* Do We Appreciate?

Who? It's definitely Peter Duryea, (and his advisor, Will Logan, Jr., a well-known writer for a weekly Chicago turf paper—the man who had advocated so strongly for the horse to be rescued from the auction).[146] Peter was eight years old when he was bought by Duryea and Stokes, and (eventually) sent to Patchen Wilkes Farm in Lexington, Kentucky; he must have truly appreciated the change from his life at Forbes Farm. Records show that Peter The Great was put to stud for the 1904 season beginning on February 9, advertised as available at a $100 stud fee, and "limited to 15 public mares".[147] (That would be similar to a stallion's owner today asking a $2,000 stud fee.)

Assume The Position

Peter The Great started in his new position as a sire at Patchen Wilkes Farm as the second month of 1904 rolled in, the "fastest trotting stallion that had ever stood [at stud] in the state" up to that time, declares Hervey, informing us that "it was the beginning of the most successful stud career in the history of trotting-horse breeding".[148] When Peter arrived in Lexington, no other stallion was fulfilling the owners' expectations as stud for the farm;[149] although Peter had made no large stud seasons prior to this, henceforth the reverse would be true. In addition to his duties with the farm's broodmares, Peter The Great was also much sought-after as a stud for outside the farm, drawing the best mares. In a December 13, 1973 article in *Harness Horse Magazine*, written half a century after Peter's death, writer Ken McCarr added his own praise to Hervey's earlier assessment of the horse, proclaiming that when Peter The Great assumed the stud position at Patchen Wilkes Farm, "thus was launched one of the most successful stud careers in the history of the sport up to the present supersires".[150]

"Share and Share Alike"

The breeding of mares "on shares", which was sometimes the case with Peter The Great, is a practice worthy of brief mention here, although the details are few. "From the beginning" of Peter's years with Stokes, Hervey explains, "the custom was followed of partnership deals, whereby especially desirable mares were bred on shares, Mr. Stokes taking over the foals if he so desired." Two examples of foals bred with this type of partnership deal were Peter's son, Peter Volo (2:02), who would become a famous stud in his own right, and his daughter Volga (2:04½) who, Hervey tells us, was "unbeaten as a race mare and a marvelous" broodmare.[151]

One Busy Horse: Peter's Stud Card Was Always Full

Peter was no wallflower, that's for sure, never lacking entries in his studbook. In the two decades that followed, wrote Hervey, Peter The Great would become a phenomenon, producing "record-breaking colt trotters, and Futurity winners in a degree hitherto unknown"[152], and do this, added Karen Greengard in her 1997 article about Peter, with amazing ruggedness and longevity, and with almost miraculous consistency. At the turn of the century, she continued, a Standardbred stallion that made creditable racehorses out of 10% of his offspring was considered a success.[153] Over the next twenty years, Peter The Great would produce foals of a quantity and quality that had never been seen in the trotting breed before.[154]

Your Place Or Mine?

Once a stallion's services had been booked for a mare, the usual practice was for a stud horse to go to the mare's farm for the breeding, rather than the other way around. It was generally believed that a mare would be more likely to "catch" if she was bred at home, as she could be kept relatively quiet after the mating—rather than being placed in a horse cart and transported back over rough dirt roads to her own farm. (Could this be how the expression *on home turf* originated?) For the trip to the mare's farm, the stallion would be harnessed to a special stud cart with four-foot tall wheels, (which made it easily distinguishable from other carts), used by a stallion's owner expressly for this purpose. Once the stallion had fulfilled his obligations, he would be harnessed to the stud cart for the trip back to his own farm. With a valuable stallion such as Peter The Great, who commanded high stud fees, it would have been different: the mare would have been brought to the stud, so as not to incur a possible injury to the stallion.[155]

They Did *NOT* Do Their Homework...

The on-going partnership between Duryea and Stokes lasted only a few more seasons, after which Stokes became Peter The Great's full owner for roughly a decade, from about 1906–1916.[156] In his article in *Hoof Beats*, Dean A. Hoffman quotes Hervey as saying that Stokes "spent little time on his farm", leaving the horses entrusted to "largely illiterate" farm hands, whose breeding records were difficult to read. The poor quality of the recordkeeping at Patchen Wilkes Farm is one reason why there are no reliable statistics on the number of offspring Peter The Great sired. (Records were so poorly kept that questions even arose regarding possible "false" Peter The Great foals.)[157] Hervey, again as quoted by Hoffman, once saw the records and declared them to be "beyond human power to either decipher or understand". Despite Peter The Great's "immense popularity", and his by then "international stature" as a stud, continued the article, Peter "was a victim of the general chaos that prevailed at Patchen Wilkes Farm during the teens". The unsavory reputation of Stokes' farm at this time, in fact, caused many breeders to decline boarding their mares at Stokes' farm.[158] All in all, the lack of direct supervision resulted in both the farm's business affairs, and its horses, suffering from neglect.

Cinderella Story, Part Two: *The Sequel*

It was "déjà vu all over again", as the saying goes. In the *Hoof Beats* article, Hoffman continues quoting, as Hervey "well recall[s]" seeing Peter The Great during that period at Patchen Wilkes Farm. Hervey expressed "astonishment and indignation" at finding Peter "in miserable shape—thin, gaunt and ragged, neglected and unkempt, his coat dry, coarse, and lusterless...yet, just as he stood, he had the highest earning capacity of any trotting sire in America". Hervey enlarges, telling us that "the owners of the nation's best brood mares were standing in line for bookings" to Peter, and that his services were in such demand that artificial insemination was "resorted to in the cases of many of them". Concluding the remarks about the poor conditions, Hoffman's article said that talk about the "disgraceful care the great patriarch suffered reached the ears of W.E.D. Stokes, who [then] had the stallion returned to prime condition".[159]

"What a Stud!"

Statistics show that a stud horse can sire 40–70 foals per season for about twenty years[160]; the miracle of artificial insemination increased that figure substantially. While Peter The Great was standing at stud at Patchen Wilkes Farm, "over one hundred brood mares" at the farm were available to him, "in addition to his outside service". "Unofficial" but "credible" sources, according to Hervey, said that while at his peak, "for half a dozen years or more", with the help of artificial insemination, "over two hundred mares were in this manner annually served by [Peter The Great]". Hervey relates, "Kentucky was filled, year after year, with the picked brood mares of the entire U.S.A., all booked to [Peter] and eagerly waiting their turn to be served, while as [when] great race mares closed their turf careers they swelled the army of his consorts". Hervey acknowledges that "the market for [Peter The Great's] yearlings could not be supplied...so excessive was the drain upon his procreative powers that it began to tell upon him perceptibly...and there were seasons when at the close [Peter] was much run down".[161]

Make Me An Offer I Can't Refuse

A sudden announcement hit the papers on February 11, 1916, stunning the trotting world: *Peter The Great had been sold!* The new owner was thirty-six year old Indianapolis banking tycoon Stoughton A. Fletcher III, and the $50,000 purchase price was "a record", Hervey states, "for a twenty-one-year-old stallion of any breed".[162] (No wonder they were stunned; incredibly, that purchase price would be a sum of over *$900,000* today.) Ten times the original $5,000 paid for the horse by Stokes' partner Duryea in the Old Glory auction, it was an offer that Stokes apparently could not refuse. Over three decades later, in a 1948 article, the *Kalamazoo Gazette* would boast that Peter The Great soon returned that purchase price, earning $55,000 in stud fees (over $1 million today) for Fletcher *in just his first year* at Fletcher's Laurel Hall Farm.[163]

Was He, Or Was He *Not?*
There are many people who maintain that Fletcher had a partner in the purchase of Peter The Great, although there is no mention of a partner in Hervey's 1947 article. (And whether 'tis better to accept that belief, or perchance to wonder if it's true: *that* is the question here.) From apparently widespread acceptance, it seems as if a wealthy and influential Indianapolis man by the name of Thomas Taggart might have been Fletcher's partner in the purchase of Peter The Great.[164] The unsubstantiated story related below appears to support this; however, not having come across any factual partnership information, we'll refer to Peter The Great's new owner as "Fletcher" for simplicity. (We'll meet Thomas Taggart again later on in Peter's tale.)

It's *"In The Bag"*
Here's the story. Late in the closing decade of the twentieth century, an old gentleman who had worked for Taggart for many years related the following tale to an admirer of Peter The Great. "While in a room at the Claypool Hotel in Indianapolis", Taggart's former employee reminisced, relating his own small part in completing the deal, "I was handed a satchel containing the entire purchase price for Peter The Great, *$50,000 in cash*, which I then delivered to another room."[165] (Fletcher and Taggart, both powerful men in Indiana, were surely acquainted; the story, if accurate, would link Taggart to the purchase in some unspecified way.)

A Kingdom For Your Horse
Why would Fletcher pay what amounted to a king's ransom for a sire of horses? An article in the August 2, 1916 edition of *The Horse Review* pronounced the $50,000 purchase price a "new record, unprecedented, even for high-priced horses". Marveling that Peter The Great was "the most prolific sire of extreme speed and [the most] successful racehorse in the history of the light harness turf", the article at the same time conceded that Peter was 21 years old, "and at that age", it stated candidly, "the career of the average great sires, if not already concluded, is something which any day may bring to an end, for such is the course of nature". The *Horse Review* article opined that "Mr. Fletcher's act represented an immense admiration for the horse", and that it was "a sentimental rather than a speculative purchase".[166] Tops among reasons for the extraordinary purchase price must have been, quite simply, Peter's colts and fillies: his offspring were becoming well known for their speed, their durability and their steadiness at the trot, and many were making their marks on the racing scene.

And The Answer Is...
"This [the reputation that was building in regards to Peter's foals] continued throughout his twelve seasons [with Stokes], and as his success as a sire began to mount", Hervey informs us, it culminated in one "unprecedented since that of Hambletonian...until at last it reached what were in effect fantastic heights."[167] Under Stokes "no limit was placed upon [Peter's] bookings, and the public demand becoming inordinate, the practice of insemination", as we learned before, "was resorted to upon a large scale". Fletcher would have been well aware of these facts: as a sire, Peter The Great was worth every penny of the high purchase price.

He'll Give You The Answer That You Endorse...
Peter The Great himself would likely have endorsed the move; his purchase by Fletcher would prove to be a good change for the horse. Peter was at first placed at stud at Forkland Farm in Lexington for the 1916-1917 seasons, "to fill engagements already booked",[168] and he would be brought up to good condition while there. Among other things, his left hock, troublesome for years, had "puffed up until it was very unsightly". At the time of Fletcher's purchase, Peter had been "by no means at his best", according to Hervey, but he "responded well to the care [now] lavished upon him".[169] Upon completion of his stud commitments in Kentucky, Peter The Great would go to Fletcher's Laurel Hall Farm in Indiana. (Reflecting later on the years 1910-1918, seven spent with Stokes and two while at Forkland Farm, Hervey tells us that "Peter [would beget] no less than 424 Standard performers" during that span, "or an average of 47 per year...a larger number than any other stallion ever begot in a single season".)[170]

51

Forgive and Forget

For thirteen years Peter The Great had been a sire at Stokes' Patchen Wilkes Farm in Lexington, and, although for some of that time he had been neglected, he had always been in great demand as a stud. At Hervey's request, measurements of Peter The Great had been taken in 1913, while Peter was still at Stokes' farm. The measurements, repeated five years later by the same person, were taken after Peter had spent two years at Forkland Farm under Fletcher's ownership, (and under the supervision of the farm's manager, Robert S. Strader). Hervey reports that the new set of figures showed that Peter the Great had not been "in such high condition in 1913 as [he would be] in 1918". For instance, his height in front, which at the first measuring was 15.3½ hands, at the second measuring was a "full 16 hands...in other words...a heavier coat of flesh had brought [nearly] an inch thicker layer of flesh over his withers".[171] Peter The Great, under Fletcher's ownership, would receive excellent care for the rest of his life.

**A thin Peter The Great,
as he appeared at Lexington, KY, before being brought to Indiana.
(Courtesy, U. S. Trotting Association)**

It Was The Good Life

Fletcher, a wealthy third-generation businessman whose Fletcher Banks dominated Indiana's financial market, built a fifty-room English Gothic mansion on the crest of a hill on his spectacular country estate outside of Indianapolis. (Wealthy he certainly was; in 1920, his bank's assets would be nearly $44 million,[172] equating to over ten times that much in present-day money.) Laurel Hall, graced by formal sunken gardens, was the perfect place for the elegant affairs the family liked to host; completed in 1916, the 40,000-square foot stone mansion had taken two years and $2 million dollars (a fabulous sum, one that would equate to well over $30 million in twenty-first century figures) to build.[173] One of the founders of the Indianapolis Speedway and the Indy 500, Stoughton Fletcher surely had some expensive cars, and a chauffeur (or two) to drive them. Fletcher also owned a private yacht, which the family used frequently for entertainment and extensive traveling.

Laurel Hall, the 40,000-square foot stone mansion built by Stoughton Fletcher, completed in 1916 at a cost of $2 million.
Supplement to the Christmas Horse Review of 1917
(Courtesy, The Harness Racing Museum & Hall of Fame)

Who's That Knock, Knock, Knocking On My Door...
Fletcher's purchase of Peter The Great back in February of 1916 had given the world of horse racing its first notion that Stoughton Fletcher, a strong racing supporter, was setting out to become a breeder of horses. By March of 1917, according to a *Horse Review* article written the following December, Fletcher had already acquired an astonishing *38 broodmares* for Laurel Hall Farm, chosen by the farm's manager, Greeley Winings, and another advisor, who displayed good judgment in selecting "not only individuals of merit, but a grandly bred lot". The article informs us that "a high standard" had been set for the mares, "the cost being entirely a secondary consideration"...the pastures at Laurel Hall provided a "veritable treat, bringing back to memory races in which...numerous of these mares themselves [had been] engaged on the Grand and other circuits", while "the dams of turf champions...were also plentifully present". Over the next nine months, an additional 11 mares were added, bringing the "number of select and famous matrons" available to knock at Peter The Great's stable door to a grand total of 47.[174]

Mr Fletcher & Colonel Ashby

Fletcher with one of Peter's sons; Laurel Hall Farm, circa 1916-1917.
Supplement to the Christmas Horse Review of 1917
(Courtesy, The Harness Racing Museum & Hall of Fame)

Laurel Hall Farm Manager Winings and Peter The Great in 1917.
Supplement to the Christmas Horse Review of 1917
(Courtesy, The Harness Racing Museum & Hall of Fame)

"Nothing But The Best!"

Fletcher's 1500-acre estate on 56th Street was located just a few miles northeast of the fairgrounds in Indianapolis. After Peter The Great's 1917 stud bookings at Forkland Farm in Kentucky had been fulfilled, Laurel Hall Farm, under the management of Greeley Winings, became Peter's home. The estate, with its excellent stables, had its own horse trainer; houses were provided for the trainer, and for the help needed to care for the horses.[175] The grounds of the estate, with its five cottages, its impressive barns and trotting track, and its pretty pastures, provided a place where Fletcher could forget his problems, "habitually stretching beneath a shade tree and taking in his Peter The Great dream world", said the *Indianapolis Star*. The move to Laurel Hall Farm marked the beginning of a new life for the horse that had, over the years, experienced more than his share of difficulties. Peter The Great was placed at the head of the stallions at Laurel Hall Farm, and would produce some of his finest sons and daughters during his six years there.[176] The farm would be Peter's home for the rest of his life.

One of the remarkable training barns
at Fletcher's 1500-acre Laurel Hall estate near Indianapolis; circa 1916-1917.
Supplement to the Christmas Horse Review of 1917
(Courtesy, The Harness Racing Museum & Hall of Fame)

As Good As It Gets

Laurel Hall Farm was at its prime when Peter The Great came to it for the 1918 season, a "splendid farm headed by the acknowledged greatest of all sires", according to *The Horse Review*, which touted it as "one of the showplaces of the Middle West—in fact, of the entire country". The farm, stocked with the best equipment, had large and roomy barns located handily at the edge of the one-mile track for the horses that were in training. The "stallion king of this grand establishment" was Peter The Great, the difficulties of his past now far behind him—a horse appreciated and valued, his superiority as a sire recognized and acknowledged at last. Gone were the days when he had been banished and mistreated. Peter The Great now had beautiful green pastures in which to graze contentedly, and a private bungalow barn all his own. Constructed especially for the king of trotting sires, the bungalow was "attractively built and parked", says Hervey[177], and was graced with blossoming flowers. (The granddaughter of Peter's trainer Johnston, when telling of a visit to Peter The Great at Laurel Hall Farm, recalled that there was even a "padded" floor in the private barn, says a *Kalamazoo Gazette* article.)[178]

Elegantly appointed bungalow home built for Peter The Great at Laurel Hall Farm; circa 1918-1923. (Courtesy, U. S. Trotting Association)

Peter The Great, in front of the bungalow home constructed especially for the king of trotting sires; Laurel Hall Farm, circa 1918-1923. (Courtesy, U. S. Trotting Association)

Give It Up For...
Peter The Great. "The latch-string is out at Laurel Hall, and all who are interested in seeing the world's greatest sire, a superb band of broodmares, and one of the grandest and most beautiful farms in the world will find a warm welcome there", proclaimed *The Horse Review* in its December 12, 1917 article. Established at Laurel Hall Farm with a large band of home-owned mares, Peter soon had no less than 44 of his own weanlings around him at the farm, many of which were from Fletcher's own mares. "Just think of it—having in one's possession this large number of weanlings by the greatest sire of all time!" raved *The Horse Review*.[179] Peter's obvious potency in 1918, at "the ripe age of twenty-three years", stated the article, provided more proof that Peter The Great was a remarkable sire: he certainly deserved the continuous accolades he received at the hands of the horse racing world.

"You're The Best Thing...That Ever Happened To Me"
During his six years at Laurel Hall Farm, Peter The Great was fortunate to be placed under the care of a fellow named Jake Councilman. Jake, who had been a trainer in his early years, found that in his mid-fifties he now much preferred the role of personal caretaker to Peter, giving him the regular exercise, the rubdowns, the grooming, all the care essential to keep the horse in good health. Admired as the possessor of a fine intellect, Jake was also well known for his faithfulness and for an unbounded energy that made his humble tasks shine. Peter The Great was described as "becoming much attached to Jake", and the feeling was reciprocated, as Jake was likewise described as being very attached to the famous trotter and sire, and "never far from his side". When talking about Peter, Jake often said that Peter The Great had "intelligence ahead of lots of human beings", and would tell stories to prove it.[180]

Jake Councilman and Peter The Great; Laurel Hall Farm, circa 1918-1923.
(Courtesy, U. S. Trotting Association)

A Little Horseplay

Peter The Great now had a fast friend, one who was loyal and true, one who would bring affection and contentment to the last years of his life. Jake must have brought Peter apples or carrots (or other things that delight a horse), putting them in the palm of his hand for Peter to nuzzle with his soft lips. At times, Peter might have been found lifting his head over the wooden gate of his stall, mischievously knocking the hat from Jake's head as the man passed by while doing his chores. Things like this were surely part of the bond forged between the horse and the man who loved him—the man who later on, when Peter died, would express the wish to have his own ashes, upon his death, scattered over Peter The Great's grave. If only we could read some of the stories Jake liked to tell about Peter; but alas, none appear to have been recorded for posterity. And—as we touched on earlier—other things were not recorded, either. Let's take a look at some statistics that *were* recorded, however.

"You're Going Down" Peter The Great Vs. Hambletonian 10

Reminiscent of a movie classic in which an unknown gets a chance to go up against a champion boxer, the "match" between Peter The Great and his ancestor Hambletonian 10 (who was revered rather like a Greek god—like Apollo, for instance) refers to the number of foals each horse sired. The match ended, perhaps, in a split decision: you must judge it for yourself. Hambletonian 10's statistics, carefully kept, are most impressive: for instance, in the 1864 stud season, at the age of fifteen, Hambletonian 10 mated with 217 mares and produced 148 foals. [181] Quoting the horse's lifetime figures, Hervey tells us that in his twenty-four seasons at stud, Hambletonian 10 covered 1,908 mares and got 1,331 foals.[182] (Note that these are simply *foals that were born*, with no regard to whether they ever raced, or won a race.)

Going For It...

Hervey, in the same 1947 article, states that "while precise figures... cannot be given for the number of mares [Peter The Great] covered and foals that resulted, it is certain they exceeded those of any other trotting sire of modern times; while it is probable that even the historic record of Hamiltonian 10...so often cited as unequaled of its kind, falls short of it".[183] If Peter The Great's record of foals sired had been properly kept over his twenty-three full seasons at stud, one can speculate that Hambletonian 10's amazing record *might* have fallen to that of Peter The Great, the descendant who shared his blood. One statistic we do know for certain about Peter The Great is that he sired 661 *record performers* (remember, only horses that actually *win* an official race are called "record performers").[184] Peter must surely have sired many other foals—foals that either didn't win official races, or that never raced at all. An article titled *"Historical Standardbred Foundation Sires"* said that Peter The Great "covered thousands of mares, and the number of his off-spring could not be determined".[185] Might the record of Hambletonian 10 have been knocked out by Peter The Great's? Because of poor record keeping...no one will ever know.

Tall Tales?

One of the elegant parties held in the Laurel Hall mansion, according to the tales, was recalled with astonishment (and some dismay). According to the story that was told, guests were said to have attended a "mating" party held on the lawn to mark the mating of Peter The Great and the mare he was to breed with. Rumor had it that a similar party was also held in the marble and paneled main hall of the mansion, an event that was said to have resulted in thousands of dollars worth of repairs to the flooring.

~ ~ ~

Another tale, often repeated, was one of Fletcher riding Peter The Great into the finely decorated drawing room of the Laurel Hall mansion, to warm up before the room's massive limestone fireplace. That room—as well as others in the gracious mansion—would have been filled with beautiful flowers grown in the estate's own private greenhouse. (That, we know, *is* true.)

Been There...
With all of the farm's broodmares lined up for him at Laurel Hall, it's certain that Peter The Great earned the title of "stallion king" that had been bestowed upon him. Just as the calendar was about to usher in a new year, information was released about Peter's outside bookings. *The Horse Review* in its December 1917 article quoted Laurel Hall Farm's manager as saying that "in 1918 we will take 25 approved outside mares for Peter The Great, all to be bred by impregnation, and the fee will be $500 [roughly $7,000 now] to guarantee a live foal". Winings went on to say that "the most modern and scientific methods of impregnation will be practiced and a veterinarian who is thoroughly familiar the process will be employed", stating with an assurance rather amusing to us now that "there is no question but that the foals are just as vigorous and in every way as capable as those that come from direct service".[186]

...Done That?
Later facts, however, seem to conflict with the details of Peter's outside bookings as recorded above. Certainly the press release by Winings would be accurate, yet Hervey's 1947 article tells us that after Peter The Great went to Laurel Hall Farm, Fletcher "limited him to [just] ten outside mares...and during the last few seasons withdrew him wholly from public service".[187] Still another article, published in 1997 by the *Michigan Harness Horseman's Association*, said that "the great sire bred full books until 1922".[188] These statements don't seem to correlate very well at first glance, until one considers that Hervey might have been speaking of a time after Peter had been at the farm for a while, and that the "full books" mentioned in the most recent article could have included the farm's own mares.

"Tell Me About it, *Stud*"
Grease your mind and slip back for a moment to the years at the turn of the century. Peter The Great was beginning his stud career then, and only sires "in the first rank" were able to command a stud fee of more than $100, according to the *Indianapolis Star*.[189] Peter The Great's stud fees "mounted with his fame, rising by stages from $100 to $1,000",[190] (in today's figures, those fees would begin at roughly $2,000 and climb to around $20,000), his $1,000 fees being "the largest then charged for a trotting sire". (With the exception, you may recall, of the exorbitant $2,500 fee that Forbes asked for Peter's limited stud season way back in 1899.)[191] Peter The Great's stud fees contributed to a very considerable profit for his owner. In a 1963 *W.M.U. News Magazine* article, author Leon W. Miller remembered talking with Laurel Hall Farm's manager Greeley Winings decades before, while at a Grand Circuit meet in Kalamazoo. Miller wrote: "Winings told me once...that when we [Winings and Fletcher] bought the horse for $50,000 most horsemen thought [they] were crazy, but in the eight years [they] had him, [Peter] made [Fletcher] a profit of $400,000."[192] The $50,000 purchase price, so tremendously high at the time, was thus returned eight times over in profit. (Putting that in perspective for us early in the twenty-first century, that profit would have been an amount surpassing $4 million.)

Rags to Riches
Peter The Great's experiences throughout a life standing at stud had taken him, in a sense, from rags with Forbes to riches with Fletcher. His career as a sire, however, had been a different story, one of more consistency. "During [Peter The Great's] entire prolonged stud career of twenty-three [full] years", according to Hervey, "he was mated with the choicest mares that America commanded." Hervey summed it up this way in his 1947 article: Peter's owners Forbes, Stokes, and Fletcher all had broodmares that "were, individually and collectively, the best that money could buy and expert selection assemble; while those sent to him by public patrons represented the crème de la crème of the entire country".[193] *Riches, indeed.*

'Peter Went To Sleep'

Due to poor investments during World War I, Fletcher's extensive realm, widely diversified in categories ranging from banking to oilfields, was trapped in a financial crisis.[194] Rumor had it that he lost over fifteen million dollars when the bottom dropped out of the sugar market in 1920. One by one, early in the decade, Fletcher's investments began to shatter and then collapsed; in 1923, he withdrew completely from the family banking business. To quote an article in the *Indianapolis Star Magazine* printed over four decades later, "his racing stable went up for auction, Laurel Hall was lost to creditors, Peter went to sleep and Fletcher slipped into obscurity".[195]

"The One Thing..."

And so, Peter went to sleep. With his head in his faithful Jake's lap, in his stall at the bungalow barn at Laurel Hall Farm, Peter The Great died suddenly, after a short illness, on March 25, 1923, at the age of twenty-eight.[196] Silence reigns in that statement—just as it did in Peter's stall that day. And with the silence comes this thought: What is the one thing that is most important in life? A decade or so ago, a classic movie about three friends who go off on a week's adventure to become cowboys addressed that very issue, as the men found themselves riding and roping their way to a greater understanding of themselves and each other. The movie brought up the "one thing" most important in each person's life--but it never told us what the one thing was. We come to realize that we must each discover it, over time, for ourselves. The "one thing", for Peter, must surely have been the devotion of Jake and the constancy of his life at Laurel Hall Farm.

Happy Trails To You...Until We Meet Again

Peter The Great had already embarked upon on another season at stud when he died, having in fact been bred with six mares already that spring—although none "got with foal".[197] His always-troublesome left hock had puffed up over time (as we know) until it was very unsightly, and during his last years the other hock had become similarly affected. Yet "he did not go lame", relates Hervey, "and to the day of his death [Peter] retained his activity and ease of movement".[198] Peter The Great was buried, according to Hervey, in front of his bungalow barn. Jake's wish to someday have his own ashes scattered over Peter's grave was well known to friends who knew both the man, and the horse that meant so much to him.[199] Jake, standing by the grave, would have said his final goodbye that day believing that, when the trail of his own life reached its end, he would be with Peter The Great again.

Tributes After Peter's Death: This Writer Could *"Talk The Talk"*

John Hervey considered Joseph I. Markey (who wrote under the pen name of 'Marque') the greatest and most versatile writer active in the sport of horse racing in the first three decades of the twentieth century, said turf writer Dean A. Hoffman in his article in *Hoof Beats*. Markey (described by Hoffman as a man who could "talk the talk") traveled extensively and came to know horses well; his opinions were both respected and requested. Shortly after Peter The Great's sudden death, Markey paid tribute to the great stallion in the pages of *The Horse Review*. Hoffman records that amongst the words Marque penned were the following: "Peter The Great is to the Standard breed of horses what Shakespeare is to literature, what Michelangelo is to art, and what Washington, Jefferson and Lincoln are to we who are devoted to the traditions of our Republic."[200] What an eloquent testimony to the life of Peter The Great.

Peter's Story Doesn't End Here

Peter The Great's story doesn't end with his death, and with his grave at Laurel Hall Farm. There are things yet to be told, and a few questions that have yet to be answered....

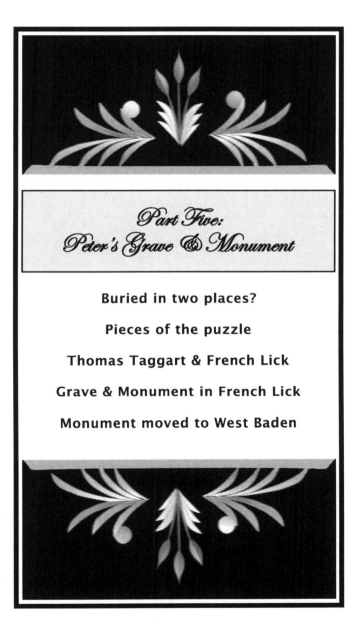

Part Five:
Peter's Grave & Monument

Buried in two places?

Pieces of the puzzle

Thomas Taggart & French Lick

Grave & Monument in French Lick

Monument moved to West Baden

On a Quest For...*Information*

Let's back up for a minute. You should know that it wasn't easy to discover where Peter The Great was buried—it was provided above for continuity of the story. But no information could be found at first. What seemed to be a very simple question developed into a quest for information, one which, surprisingly, turned out to be a quest for fun as well. Looking for the information was definitely challenging, but it *was* fun.

Talking On The Telephone...

Now, you think you already know the answer to where Peter The Great was buried—but that answer didn't come until after some phone calls had been made to Indiana, to the area where Peter had lived. And, as it turns out, that answer was not the *only* answer. The calls provided verbal information, as well as various articles about Peter The Great, and there were conflicting details: Peter seemed to have been buried at two different places. Obviously, one of them had to be wrong. More phone calls yielded the information that Peter had indeed been buried at two different places—just not at the same time. Peter The Great had been unearthed from his grave at Laurel Hall Farm and reburied in another location. *Why?* Curiosity piqued, more questions arose, and more phone calls followed.

Pieces of The Puzzle

The additional calls revealed the surprising news that there was a monument to Peter The Great, and it was at the top of Mount Aire in French Lick, Indiana. (*French Lick, Indiana? Why?*) Now that *was* news, and it was puzzling as well: Peter had been buried in an unmarked grave, but now it seemed there was a monument, (and it was *not* the one in Kalamazoo, which we'll get to later). No one in French Lick could tell when the monument had been placed there, just that it "had been there ever since anyone could remember". One article about Peter said that the American Legion had later erected a monument to Peter The Great—but it didn't tell when, or what it looked like. Another article said there was a monument at the West Baden Dome Hotel, not far from French Lick. Surely all three pieces of information couldn't be right? Ah, but it seems that they could. The effort to pinpoint the truth resulted in more phone calls, and chats with many really nice people. And each conversation added a piece to the puzzle.

The Never-Ending Story...

Here are some of the questions that by now simply could not be left unanswered, beginning first with this rather emotional one: *Would Jake's ashes ever be sprinkled on Peter's grave, as Jake wished?* Then: *When was Peter The Great unearthed and reburied? And where? And for that matter: why? And of course: What was that about a monument in French Lick?* For the answers, and Peter The Great's entire story from start to finish, (including a few short side trips by way of explanation), get yourself settled in the saddle, tighten up on the reins, and come along for the ride...

"Make Your Choice..."

There are some people who like to ferret out a mystery and hear all the details, and some who just like to cut to the chase. There are a lot of quite interesting and definitely colorful bits of information coming up that you may not want to miss. The "details" person will surely enjoy the trip, so read on. The "chase" person can always head to the top of page 68 for the answers to the questions about both Peter's remains and the monument in French Lick. For the short ride back to Kalamazoo, (if you must), head to page 73.

63

"Takes a Licking and..."

How did French Lick get its an unusual name? The "French" part was from the early French traders who discovered mineral springs bubbling from the ground. And the area really *did* take a licking—its mineral and salt licks did, that is. These deposits, on the ground and rocks in French Lick's hilly areas, drew an abundance of wildlife who came, literally, to lick them, somehow knowing that their bodies needed salt to ensure survival.

~ ~ ~

French Lick later became a rest stop for settlers and their cattle heading west. By the late 1800's, people began to recognize the potential of the area's natural mineral springs, and flocked to soak in them, believing that the waters could cure anything from alcoholism to constipation. French Lick's natural spring water, which stank of sulfur, was marketed (quite successfully) for its curative powers; the drink was named "Pluto Water" after the god of the underworld from which it escaped. (As to its usefulness in helping with constipation, it was said that the advertisements for the water, which included the phrase "When Nature Won't, Pluto Will", were definitely *not* an exaggeration.)

The Higher They Are, The Farther They May Fall

We must return to Laurel Hall Farm, where Peter The Great was buried, to start our trip. Fletcher's far-flung realm lay in ruins, due largely to the poor investments during World War I we touched on earlier. In response to an urgent appeal by the War Department, Fletcher had purchased two companies and converted both to the manufacture of marine turbine engines—without properly analyzing the risks, and unwisely using all of his personal assets to finance the effort. When the war ended earlier than expected, government contracts were abruptly cancelled; that, combined with the post-war financial depression and a general slump in business, contributed greatly to the disintegration of Fletcher's empire.[201]

~ ~ ~

Due to mounting financial pressures, Fletcher had given up his controlling interest in the family bank in 1921; that same year, he lost his wife to suicide. As has already been stated, Fletcher severed his banking connections completely in 1923; the following year, he filed for bankruptcy, listing debts in an amount approaching $2 million (like $22 million today, keep in mind) and assets of less than $500 (roughly $5,500 now). Ownership of his estate reverted to the bank he had once led.[202] According to Ken McCarr's article in *Harness Horse Magazine* in December of 1973, "when Fletcher had to dispose of his horses, the farm was purchased by Thomas D. Taggart".[203] Fletcher and his teenage children left Indiana, moving first to Florida, it was said, and then, soon after, to California, thus passing out of our story.

Here's The Scoop

At last we've arrived at how French Lick comes into the story about Peter. Thomas Taggart was now said to be owner of the Laurel Hall Farm, where Peter The Great lay in his simple grave. Two decades before Peter's death, shortly after the turn of the century, Taggart and a group of men had purchased 350 acres and built a hotel in French Lick, Indiana, (an area located roughly sixty miles north of the Kentucky border), replacing an earlier hotel that had been destroyed by fire.[204] Taggart, a staunch Irish Democrat, had long been one of the most influential men in the state of Indiana, one who—among other things—had been the mayor of Indianapolis from 1895 to 1901, and Chairman of the Democratic National Committee from 1900 to 1908.

Thomas D. Taggart
Photo of portrait (circa 1920's) taken by the author
(Courtesy, West Baden Dome Hotel)

Up In The Air at Mount Aire

Peter The Great's monument was (or *had been*, as the phone calls revealed; we'll get to that later) "up on Mount Aire, on the grounds of the former Thomas Taggart estate" in French Lick. The heights of Mount Aire, the second highest elevation in the state, could be seen from Taggart's hotel in French Lick, "above the hotel, not far as the crow flies". Sometime after 1925, Taggart began building a mansion at the top of Mount Aire. (The name was derived from the Latin word "aerie", which means "a dwelling on a height".) The dwelling, with its breathtaking view of the countryside, its four white columns gracing the front entrance, its offset wings, and of course, its stables, was finished in 1929 at a cost of $150,000. (The mansion, which would have cost over $1.5 million to erect today, was reportedly being built for Taggart's son. Taggart would not live to see his family in the structure: he died in the spring of 1929, before it was completed. Taggart's son and family occupied the mansion for nearly a quarter of a century, remaining until they sold the French Lick Hotel, somewhere around 1954.)

Taggart mansion on Mt. Arie, overlooking French Lick, Indiana.
Photo by Tom Roach in 1986.
(Courtesy, Indiana Standardbred Hall of Fame)

"Can't Get No...Satisfaction:" *Michigan's Horsemen*
While Taggart was up in the aire regarding the construction of the mansion in French Lick, Peter The Great still rested quietly in a (reportedly) roped-off area outside his bungalow barn at Laurel Hall Farm. There was nothing, no headstone, to show where this famous horse was buried, and so it remained, Hervey tells us, for "some years".[205] Harness historian Ken McCarr tells us that "the unmarked grave did not sit well" with loyal horsemen in Michigan, and there was once an "attempt to have Peter The Great's remains exhumed" and brought back to the city of Kalamazoo for reburial near his foaling place.[206] Unfortunately, the attempt petered out.

French Lick Had Its Share of *"Give" And "Get"*
We know that a monument to Peter The Great was at the top of Mount Arie. Looking for clues as to *why* a monument was there, some fascinating facts about French Lick came to light. For nearly 50 years, beginning with the last quarter of the 19th century, the springs and resorts at French Lick had been the playground of the rich and famous, with elite visitors like Lana Turner, Bing Crosby, Abbott & Costello, Steve Allen, Helen Keller, Nelson Rockefeller, the DuPonts, the Studebakers, and boxer Joe Louis among the guests. (You probably found that list entertaining; we're wagering that you'll find the next part quite interesting as well.) Shortly after Taggart's resort was built at the turn of the century, at roughly the same time that Peter The Great was setting out on his stud career, French Lick began to attract a different class of visitors to its newest source of income: *illegal gambling*. French Lick became the "gambling and laxative Mecca of America", and was eventually home to at least six casinos.[207] (This illegal gambling, by the way, usually caused more people to fall into the "give" category than into the "get".)

"Ten Dollar Bills Piled Three Feet High"
Although illegal, the gambling brought much excitement and plenty of money, chills and thrills to the area—along with, not surprisingly, a tougher type of visitor: gangsters such as the infamous Al Capone of Chicago.[208] During its heyday, which roughly coincided with Peter The Great's stud career, ten to fourteen trains a day stopped in French Lick; at least one railroad had run a spur down from Chicago. The approximately ninety-year old former Taggart employee mentioned earlier recalled harnessing up a team of horses and "taking the surrey down to meet the train every Friday like clockwork". Visitors climbed aboard, headed to the hotels, or to the gambling halls where "ten-dollar bills were piled three feet high on the tables", according to the old fellow. (For a while, since Taggart was extremely active in politics, his French Lick Springs resort was even said to be a sort of "unofficial national Democratic Party headquarters".)[209] Business was outstanding—until the stock market crashed in October of 1929. In a matter of days, the hotels were empty.

A Real *"Who-Dun-It?"*
The Depression years ensued, and back in Indianapolis, still there was no headstone, nothing to mark the grave of Peter The Great; yet all the while, his children, and *their* children, were making marks of another kind in the world of horse racing. Attempts were made to rectify that situation, and it seems as if they were eventually successful. John Hervey's 1947 article, (received as a result of one of those interesting phone calls), written more than two decades after Peter's death, relates the following story: "his [Peter's] home was in a bungalow...in front of which he was buried, his grave being marked by a monument erected some years later by the American Legion, which purchased Laurel Hall as one of its national homes".[210] When contacted by phone for verification, the American Legion of Indiana was most willing to assist, but was unable to find anything to support Hervey's statement that Laurel Hall had been one of their national homes—or that the Legion had been involved in erecting the monument. Nevertheless, Hervey's article definitely states that Peter The Great did get his headstone, (Ken McCarr wrote in *Harness Horse Magazine* that it was in the mid-1930's),[211] and that it marked his grave at Laurel Hall Farm.

Your Guess Is As Good As Mine...

The monument to Peter The Great, high up on Mount Aire, had obviously been commissioned by someone who held Peter in great esteem. The wording on the front of the four-foot tall granite headstone is couched in words of high praise, and a raised, side-on view of Peter The Great graces its back. Who cared enough about Peter The Great to choose the words that would forever immortalize this great horse in stone, and chose also to have Peter's silhouette etched on the back? Could this tombstone be what Hervey was referring to, when he wrote that a monument marked the grave of Peter The Great in front of the bungalow barn at Laurel Hall Farm in Indianapolis? Logic dictates that it likely is; but, as Hervey did not describe it, and as there is no evidence to either confirm or deny it, the origin of the monument—and how and when it was placed on Mount Aire—remains a mystery.

Peter The Great's monument at the former Taggart estate on Mt. Arie
in French Lick, Indiana; both pictures taken in 1986.
Photo on the left shows front view of the monument with the Taggart mansion set high on the hill at the end of the winding road. Shot on the right shows the fine workmanship of Peter The Great's raised image engraved on the back of the monument.
(Photos by Tom Roach. Courtesy, Indiana Standardbred Hall of Fame)

Ashes To Ashes, and...

One piece of the puzzle did fit neatly into place, and answered our question regarding Jake. According to a handwritten notation of a date on an otherwise undated article (given by Jake's sister to a resident of French Lick during a trip to see Peter The Great's monument), the end of the trail came to Jake Councilman in the winter of 1939.[212] Jake, who (according to the penciled note) would have been 72 years old at the time of his death, had left instructions in his will that he be cremated, and his ashes scattered over Peter's grave. According to Hervey, Jake's good friend Will Gahagan, a sportswriter who knew Peter as well, fulfilled Jake's longtime wish.[213] Sixteen years had passed since Peter had breathed his last in his stall at Laurel Hall Farm. Peter The Great and Jake Councilman were together again.

In The Meantime, Back at The Farm...

Within a few years after Peter The Great's death, the Laurel Hall property had become home to Ladywood, a Catholic school for girls. Later, the verdant and rambling grounds were also the location of Cathedral High School.[214] (Later still, condominiums were built on the property; after that, in the mid–1980's, Laurel Hall became home to the Hudson Institute, a "think tank".) But we need to step back from the future now, back to the early 1950's, when the Laurel Hall estate passed into the hands of a real estate firm owned by a man named Warren Atkinson. "In subsequent years", wrote the *Indianapolis Star Magazine* in 1968, "much of the land adjoining Ladywood surrendered to the bulldozer as houses sprang up". Inevitably, somewhere around 1962, the grave of Peter The Great met a more concrete threat: "The ashes had lain for nearly 40 years", related Atkinson in the 1968 article about Peter The Great, "when a street would have run right over his grave."[215]

Move It Or Lose It

With the imminent threat of a road being paved over Peter The Great's grave, Atkinson, feeling he was "responsible for Peter's resting place", said the *Indy Star* article, decided to move the remains. He would transport them to an estate he'd acquired just a few years before—the estate of Thomas Taggart on Mount Aire, in French Lick. Now at last the reason for the "buried in two places, just not at the same time" part of the story has been unearthed.

Head, Heart, and Hooves

The phone calls mentioned earlier had yielded some additional and quite surprising information about the remains of Peter The Great. It seems that, in some parts of the country, it is tradition to bury just the head, heart and hooves of a racehorse, "the three most important parts" of a racehorse. And that is just how Peter The Great had been buried outside his bungalow barn on that day in early spring, way back in 1923.

It Behooved Them To Remove Them...

In utter simplicity, the remains of Peter The Great, sealed in a 50–gallon steel drum, were brought up into the light of day. They had been in the earth at Laurel Hall Farm for nearly four decades; traces of Jake's ashes, which had mingled with the soil as the seasons passed, would linger still in the earth that clung to the container. From the grounds of what had been Laurel Hall Farm in Indianapolis, Peter's remains were transported by pickup truck the hundred or so miles to the estate near French Lick, "bones shift[ing] gently, unseen, unheard, as the barrel rocked to and fro in the back of the speeding truck", wrote the *Indianapolis Star Magazine*.

"I'm Gonna Take You Higher..."

The remains of Peter The Great were buried on the former Taggert estate, high up on Mount Arie, overlooking French Lick and the countryside spread out below. For years afterwards, through two more owners, both the horse and the monument were on the same property—although it is not generally known if the monument actually marked the grave. Peter The Great has slept on the grounds of the privately owned estate for close to half a century now.

Spurred On To Look For The Monument

With the curiosity regarding the *two* graves of Peter The Great now laid to rest, the question of the three different locations of Peter's monument in Indiana moved to the forefront. We've already speculated about the monument on Mount Aire being the one mentioned by Hervey. (If it was, perhaps Atkinson moved it when he moved Peter The Great's remains, and it just wasn't mentioned in the article?) Be that as it may, the passage of years had affected the monument overlooking the valley as the twentieth century drew to a close. This dilemma was discovered in the summer of 1997, when an out-of-town admirer of Peter The Great set out to visit the monument he had read about in a horse racing magazine.

"It Wasn't Pretty"

Stopping at the newspaper office in French Lick for directions to the monument, the visitor was sent on a five or six mile drive on the winding one-lane road up to the top of Mount Aire. Peter's monument was located, he'd been told, at the 'Y' in the road, where the left fork went back to the stables, and the right fork led up to the mansion. And it was there that he found the monument—with difficulty, however, as it was almost completely hidden by discarded cardboard and other things, due to accidental carelessness by workers completing a remodeling project. Over the years, time had taken its toll on the monument. The centennial year of Peter The Great's birth had occurred just two years before, in 1995. It had dawned on a headstone whose once-proud stance had bowed to the demands of gravity, its granite finish weather beaten and flaking, its lettering difficult to read. Forgotten by most, nearly hidden in the tall grass, the monument was viewed with dismay by the man who stood before it, a man well aware of Peter The Great's racing wins, and of his reputation as a great trotting sire.

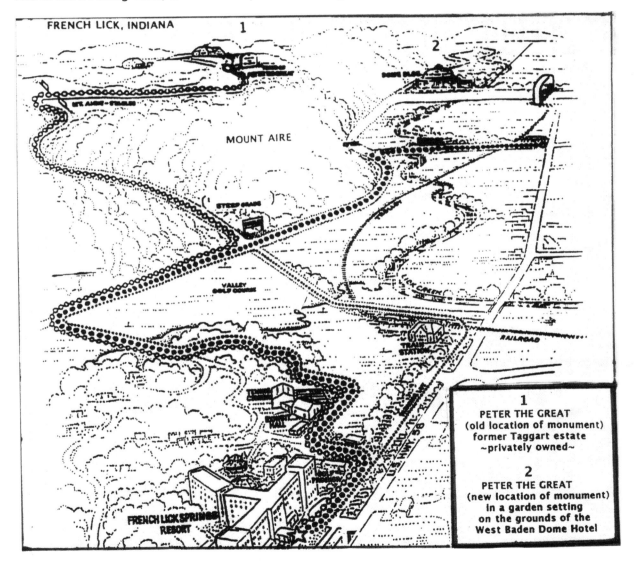

Map of the French Lick and West Baden area, marking both the old and the new (1997) location of the monument of Peter The Great. Peter's remains are buried on the grounds of the former Taggart estate, after having been moved there from Laurel Hall Farm in Indianapolis sometime around 1962.
(Map, courtesy of the French Lick Springs Resort, has been adapted as shown.)

You *Can* Make a Difference...

Concerned about the condition of the monument (and because the estate was about to be listed for sale), the fellow made a few inquiries, and brought the headstone's plight to the attention of Margie Hill, then Chairman of the Indiana Standardbred Hall of Fame. Margie in turn contacted Bill and Gayle Cook of the Cook Group; soon the Historic Landmarks Foundation of Indiana was brought into the picture. It's amazing what can be accomplished when there is a genuine wish to make things happen, combined with the financial resources to see them to completion. Permissions were obtained, steps planned, decisions made, help provided by many along the way—with the result that, by autumn of the same year, the monument of Peter The Great had been moved from its longtime home on Mount Arie, beautifully restored, and placed in a garden setting created especially for it at the West Baden Dome Hotel (perhaps three miles from Mount Aire).[216]

The (Not So) Secret Garden

No secrets about this garden (unlike the garden in a book written in 1911, when Peter The Great, then sixteen years old, was more than a decade into the stud career that would make him one of the most famous trotting sires of all time). The monument's new home on the grounds of the West Baden Dome Hotel is anything but secret. The hotel location was chosen specifically to allow greater access to the monument, so that it could be seen and appreciated by many, thus preserving the memory of Peter The Great.

~ ~ ~

There is something almost magical about a walled garden, and, although the walls of the path leading up to and around the monument are short and composed of flagstone, the garden in the wooded area where Peter The Great's monument now stands is no exception. Flowers of all colors bloom in the spring, touched by the sun that filters through the shade of the nearby trees, filling the peaceful glade with light. In fall, leaves drift slowly down to rest on the grass, or to float on the mirrored surface of the small pond hidden a few feet from the monument.

Peter The Great's monument seen here
in its new location at the West Baden Dome Hotel
near French Lick, Indiana. Monument restored and moved here in 1997.
(Photos by Nat Hill. Courtesy, Indiana Standardbred Hall of Fame)

The Horse Whisperers...

Whispers can almost be heard, echoing in the breeze that stirs the trees around the monument. Whispers, perhaps, of those like Jake, who knew Peter The Great as a famous sire, or whispers of those who knew him during his brief but shining career as a racehorse—or even of those who knew him as a foal, when he frisked in the paddock near the oak trees of his birthplace at The Oaklands in Kalamazoo, Michigan, over a century ago. Faint hints of the echoes are in the breeze that moves through the wooded area, caressing both facades of the beautifully restored monument, lingering for a moment on the words inscribed on the front, which proudly proclaim Peter The Great's name and accomplishments—touching now on the back, where the silhouette of the famous horse is etched, plainly visible to those who know to look. We can almost hear the voices of those who stand there today, reading the words, and marveling at the records of this famous horse:

PETER THE GREAT

2:07¼

1895-1923

661 RECORD PERFORMERS

SIRE OF

DAMS OF 971 RECORD PERFORMERS

BY SHEER MERIT HE LIFTED HIS NAME TO THE HEAD OF ALL TROTTING PROGENITORS. DEATH LEFT HIM UNRIVALLED BY ONE OF HIS OWN BREED REGARDLESS OF ERA, AGE, OR BREEDING.

"A Better Place To Be"

Peter The Great's monument now stands in a garden area at the West Baden Dome Hotel. Built as a luxury hotel in 1902, the hotel, which has been called the "Eighth Wonder of the World", was named for its gorgeous glass and steel domed atrium. (The dome, ten feet larger than the dome at St. Peter's in Rome, remained the world's largest clear-span dome until the 1960's, when the Houston Astrodome was built.)

~ ~ ~

After the Depression hit in 1929, business was gone, and the building was sold to Jesuits, who kept it for thirty years. Abandoned for a time after 1983, the structure would eventually suffer neglect and come close to collapse. The hotel, named a National Historic Landmark in 1987, has not functioned as such for many years, but will be taking guests again in 2007, once restorations estimated at $34 million have been completed under the guidance of the Cook Group, an Indiana-based business. The Historic Landmarks Foundation of Indiana, which purchased the property in 1996, provides tours of the hotel and grounds seven days a week.

***West Baden Dome Hotel
(Photo in 2005 by the author)***

Part Six:
Honors & Accolades

Kalamazoo again

Testimonials to Peter The Great

Honoree in three Halls of Fame

Monument in Kalamazoo

Corralling the facts

The Life of Peter The Great:
Herein Lies The Tail

Let's End Up Back Where We Started

We'll head back now to where it all began, to the frame barn at The Oaklands in Kalamazoo. Who could have known, on the day Peter was foaled in 1895, that no other horse would have a greater influence on the Standardbred breed as it is today than the little bay horse named Peter The Great? Who could have guessed that Peter's offspring would come to dominate the world of harness horse racing, a domination that would span the twentieth century which dawned soon after his birth, and continue into the century that followed? Michigan-bred Peter The Great, foaled to a dam born in Michigan, sired by a stallion from Battle Creek, raised in the city of Kalamazoo, has a unique place in American trotting history.[217]

A Young Peter The Great
(Courtesy, Western Michigan University Archives and Regional History Collections)

"If At First You Don't Succeed, Try, Try Again..."

Reflecting on Peter The Great's life, this old saying certainly describes his early years; in fact, one could almost say it became his mantra. Peter had a good (though definitely demanding) life with trainer Johnston during his years at Daniel Streeter's horse farm in Kalamazoo, learning to trot when he was a yearling, then learning again, twice more, before he was ready for his first race as a two-year old. And yet *again*, before he was considered ready the following year for the three-year old Futurity, which he would win by twenty lengths, stunning the racing world. After that—well, his life took a different path.

"It Was The Best of Times; It Was The Worst of Times"

The opening phrase of a famous tale of two cities (written nearly four decades before Peter The Great was born) applies without a doubt to the twists and turns that the young horse's life took as he left the good life in Kalamazoo behind him, and moved to Forbes Farm in New England. His troubles began when training began; the triumphs he had during his first and only racing season at Forbes Farm ended in disappointment, a forerunner of the troubles he would experience before long. The mistreatment and neglect Peter suffered during his nearly five years with Forbes came to an end with the rise of his famous daughter Sadie Mac, whose impact on the racing world gave Forbes the nudge he needed to dispatch Peter The Great to the Old Glory auction in New York.

"Now, Wa-a-a-it a Minute..."
After Peter's purchase by Duryea at the auction, and once he had finally been sent to Stokes' Patchen Wilkes Farm, it seemed as if things had changed for the better for Peter The Great. There would come a period, however, when the path circled back again to hard times, and when that happened, Peter rode the rough patches as well as he could. During the nearly thirteen years he spent with Stokes, and in spite of the obvious problems at the farm, Peter The Great's career as a sire became well established, his successes well known. The demand for his services was great, and his acknowledged superiority as a stud was fast on the way to making him a legend in his own time.

When You Wish Upon a Star, Makes No Difference Where You Are...
Perhaps, if Peter was still out in the paddock of an evening when twilight drew near and the stars appeared in the sky above Patchen Wilkes Farm, he might have wished for things that he somehow knew were missing in his life. Peter The Great would find that, at least for him, it *does* make a difference where you are. Peter's sale to Stoughton Fletcher would bring great change to the horse's life, as the path he now trod led him to Laurel Hall Farm, to the lasting friendship of Jake Councilman, and, ultimately, to Peter The Great's "best of times".

"You're One In a Million..."
The hit song of a congenial movie released a few years ago mirrors the life and legacy of Peter The Great. "You're one in a million", the lyrics declare, "you're once in a lifetime." Dean A. Hoffman, reflecting on the centennial of Peter The Great's birth for the U. S. Trotting Association's *Hoof Beats*, wrote the following about Peter in 1995: "The horse that was born over a century ago...may rightly lay claim to the title of the most important Standardbred of the 20th century. The story of the Standardbred in [that] century, and how the breed evolved and improved, is really the story of Peter The Great's influence. He is the fountainhead [the principal source] of trotting."[218] One in a million he certainly was: in Peter The Great, we discover above us one of the brightest stars in the history of harness horse racing.

Living Legend
Peter The Great, said to be lacking a "balanced" (both sire and dam selected with great care as to lineage) pedigree was not a horse likely to have been chosen for greatness, but he became a legend even in his own lifetime. His success as a racehorse—and particularly as a sire—bears mute testimony to the fact that no one, whether animal or human, should be pre-judged by what he is or by the circumstances from which he comes: each should be given a chance to do what he can with what lies within him. Within Peter assuredly lay the makings of greatness. He was a horse that, according to an April 1977 article in the *Michigan Harness Horseman* detailing the roots of Peter The Great, "would become the most successful progenitor that the trotting breed had produced since Hambletonian 10 himself".[219]

MHHA Chooses Peter The Great As Its "Horse of The Century"
As the twentieth century unfolded, and his legend grew, Peter The Great became known as "both inheritor and progenitor of the most important sire lines" in trotting history, as Karen Greengard so aptly phrased it in her 1997 article in *Michigan Harness Horseman*. A tribute to this exceptional horse came just as that century was about to make the turn into a new millennium, when in 1999 Peter The Great was voted "Horse of the Century" by the membership of the Michigan Harness Horseman's Association.

"And The Winner Is..."
The winner of our tale? Why, it's Peter, hands down (16 hands, to be specific). Peter The Great, says Hoffman, was gifted with such extraordinary genetic powers that he was able to pass along both his trotting power and his staying power to his progeny. Peter's monument in Indiana proclaims that the great progenitor sired 661 record performers, (498 trotters and 163 pacers), all winners of official races. It also proudly states that the daughters Peter sired would themselves bear 971 record performers on the racing scene, of whom Hervey says 117 were in the 2:05 list and 7 in the 2:00 list.[220]

SIRES

TEN LEADING SIRES OF STANDARD PERFORMERS

→ Peter the Great, 4, 2:07¼, by Pilot Medium 1597	662
Guy Axworthy, 4, 2:08¾, by Axworthy, 3, 2:15½	438
San Francisco 2:07¾, by Zombro 2:11	318
Peter Volo, 4, 2:02, by Peter the Great, 4, 2:02	290
Trampfast, 2, 2:12¼, by The Tramp 33343	282
Allerton 2:09¼, by Jay Bird 5060	271
Belwin, 4, 2:06¾, by McKinney 2:11¼	253
Bingen 2:06¼, by May King 2:20	252
General Watts, 3, 2:06¾, by Axworthy, 3, 2:15½	249
The Exponent 2:11¾, by Bingen 2:06¼	244

TEN LEADING SIRES OF STANDARD TROTTERS

→ Peter the Great, 4, 2:07¼, by Pilot Medium 1597	498
Guy Axworthy, 4, 2:08¾, by Axworthy, 3, 2:15½	402
San Francisco 2:07¾, by Zombro 2:11	259
General Watts, 3, 2:06¾, by Axworthy, 3, 2:15¼	217
Bingara 34707, by Bingen 2:06¼	216
Peter Volo, 4, 2:02, by Peter the Great, 4, 2:02	211
Allerton 2:09¼, by Jay Bird 5060	210
The Harvester 2:01, by Walnut Hall 2:08¼	200

The January 1931 edition of "The Horse Review" shows the Top Ten Leading Sires of Both Standard Performers and Standard Trotters. Peter The Great heads the list for both. (Courtesy, Western Michigan University Archives and Regional History Collections)

"Looks Like He Made It..."
The title of a classic 1977 song written by a native New Yorker could have been written especially for Peter. Peter The Great has the honor of having been inducted into three horse racing halls of fame, attesting to the extraordinary place that he occupies in American harness racing history. Peter The Great also has the distinction of having been selected as one of ten trotters chosen by the National Hall of Fame of the Trotter in Goshen, New York, in its first inductee year, as well as being one of the first horses named to its renowned Hall of Immortals.

Peter The Great: Honoree in Three Halls of Fame

National Hall of Fame of the Trotter in Goshen, NY, inducted in 1953

Michigan Harness Racing Hall of Fame, Okemos, MI, inducted in 1986

Indiana Standardbred Hall of Fame in Anderson, IN, inducted in 1993

**Peter The Great
has been honored in the
Hall of The Immortals at The Harness Racing Museum & Hall of Fame
Goshen, New York**

This is an image of a section of the Hall of Immortals at The Harness Racing Museum & Hall of Fame in Goshen New York. Since 1953, PETER THE GREAT has been a member of this illustrious group of people and horses. His achievements are so significant he was one of the first Immortals to be so named. His name appears on an opaque board, that details the dates of his birth and death. The boards line the entire perimeter of the Hall's display cases. Those elected to the Living Hall of Fame are recognized with lifelike statuettes. When the subject dies the statuette is relocated to the Hall of The Immortals. Indepth information and images of Immortals are accessed from a computer kiosk not shown in this picture.

The Immortals were formed in 1953 to recognize significant achievements and contributions to the sport of Harness Racing. The first induction class was: Axworthy, Dan Patch, Goldsmith Maid, Guy Axworthy, PETER THE GREAT, Peter Volo, Hambletonian, Joe Patchen, Single G, and Star Pointer. Humans weren't nominated and elected until 1958.

For more information on the Peter D. Haughton Hall of The Immortals, its members and the programs and services of The Harness Racing Museum & Hall of Fame please visit www.harnessmuseum.com or contact the director at POB 590, 240 Main Street, Goshen, NY 10924: 845.294.6330.

**(Photo and information about the Hall of The Immortals provided in 2005 by
The Harness Racing Museum & Hall of Fame in Goshen, New York)**

Peter The Great's name (listed under "1953", the year he was inducted) can be seen by looking closely at the arrows on the reflective surface of the Plaque in the Hall of The Immortals.
(Courtesy, The Harness Racing Museum & Hall of Fame in Goshen, New York)

His Legend Lives On...

Peter The Great's legend lives on, in the minds of those who know about his life, in the stories that have been written about him, and in the words chosen for his two monuments. The second monument commemorating Peter The Great is located in Kalamazoo, Michigan, where it marks the birthplace of the famous horse on the Streeter farm. The monument, erected in 1931, says the *Kalamazoo Gazette*, with funds provided by Streeter's daughter (by then Mrs. Fannie Jackson), his brother (Milford B. Streeter of New York), and area businessman Charles B. Hays, was placed near the barn where Peter The Great had been foaled nearly four decades before.[221] Long-time Kalamazoo residents may remember that, for a time, the Gateway and Arcadia Brook Golf Courses were on what had been the Streeter estate; the monument was then located at the northwestern corner of the Arcadia Brook Golf Course on U.S. 12 (now Stadium Drive), somewhere near VandeGiessen Road. In 1944, roughly a dozen years after Peter's monument had been commissioned, the land was purchased by Western Michigan University; the monument has been moved several times as the campus has grown.

Etched In Stone

We've roped together all of the facts regarding the site of Peter The Great's monument in Kalamazoo, so that it can be easily located. The monument, a large gray stone boulder about four feet high and somewhat triangular in shape, has been placed once again near the original site of the barn; it can be found on the east side of W. Michigan Avenue, across the street from Western Michigan University's Bernhard Center. Although the view of the monument (from the front of the Center) is partly hidden by a tall pine tree, it can easily be found. Head east from the front door of the building, cross W. Michigan Avenue, and walk towards the WMU Administration Building. The boulder (located west of that building, between it and McCracken Hall, and not far from the edge of S. Hayes Drive) bears a bronze plaque. The words on the plaque, besides noting the names of his owner and his trainer, memorialize Peter The Great's record-breaking time of 2:07¼, achieved in September of 1899 at the one-mile Empire City Track in New York. It is Peter The Great's lifetime best.

**Monument to Peter The Great located near the WMU Administration Building.
(Photo taken in 2005 by the author)**

***This image shows
Peter The Great's monument
in 1931, nestled in its terraced garden
setting near The Oaklands
in Kalamazoo, Michigan.***

(Used with the permission of the KALAMAZOO GAZETTE)

According to a December 1940 article in the Kalamazoo Gazette, "twenty thousand horse-lovers annually make the pilgrimage to Kalamazoo to stand in reverence before the great stone which marks the birthplace of Peter The Great, one of the country's most famous sires". The Gazette went on to state that the "shrine to this great horse is becoming more and more a vacation mecca for visitors to Michigan".[222]

This One's For You, Wherever You Are

Peter The Great is not buried in Kalamazoo, but he is with us nonetheless. Peter's presence can still be felt while visiting the monument on the grounds of what was once the 600-acre Streeter estate. Now, it's true that the estate where Peter lived over a century ago has been the property of Western Michigan University for many years—and it's also true that many imposing university buildings are scattered around the area. But if you visit the setting in early morning or in early evening (when there are few students around) and stand before the monument, you can almost feel the years slip away, drawing you back with them into the past, as you read the simple words that are engraved on the bronze plaque:

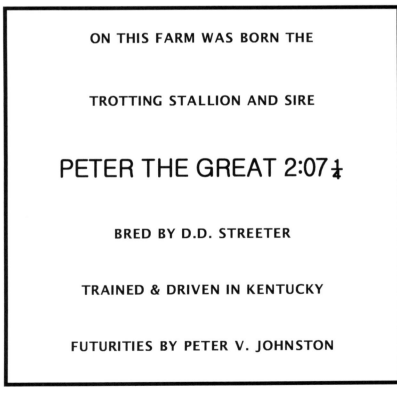

ON THIS FARM WAS BORN THE

TROTTING STALLION AND SIRE

PETER THE GREAT 2:07¼

BRED BY D.D. STREETER

TRAINED & DRIVEN IN KENTUCKY

FUTURITIES BY PETER V. JOHNSTON

An Aura of History...

The words of the monument seem to linger in the silence, and you find yourself looking around, almost as if seeking a glimpse of Peter The Great himself. If you return to the sidewalk adjacent to the street, stroll just a bit north, and look to the east, you will see The Oaklands. Gazing across the wide expanse of lawn, your glance falls on the beautiful Italianate villa set back from the road, visible through the stately oak trees that have given it shelter for many a year. And you realize that this is The Oaklands—the mansion in which the Streeter family had lived over a century ago—the mansion to which Streeter and Johnston had returned, after leading Peter The Great, head held high, from the train on the day of the triumphant homecoming from the 1898 Kentucky Futurity. Kalamazooans had greeted Peter The Great that day with the reception due a world record-breaking horse; shouts and cheers, laughter and happy tears had echoed through the grounds, as friends gathered to celebrate at The Oaklands.

The Oaklands
(Photo taken in 2005 by the author)

...and a Sense of *Mystery*

The sense of being drawn back in time, the subtle aura of history that surrounds the grounds of The Oaklands, brings with it a sense of mystery. So much time has passed. Standing there in the shade of the trees, you find yourself wondering: the barn in which Peter had been foaled—could it still be standing? And Peter The Great himself: now that all is said and done, looking back over the many years that have passed, could his influence as a sire—extraordinary as it had been years ago—still be important today? Good questions; for the answers, we'll start where Peter did—in the barn.

→ → Arrows ← ← Point the Way To Where The Barn Once Stood

The barn itself has been gone now for over half a century, but its location has not been forgotten, as can be seen from the picture below. In 1944, when the property including The Oaklands had been purchased by Western Michigan College (now WMU), the barn that had once housed the famous Peter The Great was torn down, as was the tenant and servant's house and other outbuildings of the farm, to allow for expansion by the college. The log cabin playhouse that Streeter had built for his grandchildren stood until 1959, when it too was demolished. For a time, The Oaklands became home to two of the university's presidents, Paul V. Sangren and James W. Miller. Since 1975, the university has used the mansion for small meetings and receptions, its stateliness and imposing presence reminding its visitors—and passing students— of a bygone era.[223]

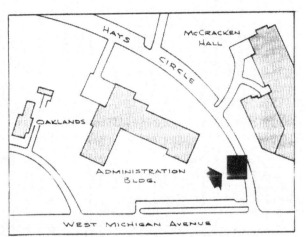

Peter the Great's birthplace is shown by the arrow in the left picture, and in relation to present campus buildings at the right.

Arrow shows location of Peter The Great's birthplace on the Streeter Farm (left);
arrow (right, on a campus map) points out the corresponding area
bounded by the Administration Building and McCracken Hall.
(Barn was also near Siedschlag Hall, not shown on map.)
(Courtesy, Western Michigan University Archives and Regional History Collections)

Corralling Our Facts About *'The Peters'*

"Books have been written about [Peter The Great], and the turf journals have carried thousands of pages about him", wrote Leon W. Miller in 1963[224], pages which have recounted the life of this extraordinary horse and the legacy seen in the racing records of his many famous offspring. Marque, the writer described by Hervey[225] as "the most brilliant as well as authoritative and well-informed writer" about harness racehorses for thirty years, wrote about Peter's progeny in the obituary he composed in honor of the great trotting sire. "Tremendous class [has been] displayed by the Peters", Hervey quoted Marque as saying about Peter's progeny, progeny who "have constitutions such as no other breed can rival." Marque continues with "even when lame, as numerous of them were when racing in high form, they kept right on winning, a trait that has often caused wonder among horsemen". Marque also wrote the simple yet descriptive comment that when racing "after their accustomed manner", the Peters tried "as if for [their lives]". Karen Greengard, in her 1997 article in the *Michigan Harness Horseman,* said that Peter The Great's offspring have been famous for their gameness, for the durability they have displayed as they have withstood the rigors of long racing campaigns, and for their steadiness at the trot.[226] Let's take a look at an amazing array of facts about Peter The Great and his influence as a sire.

Part Seven:
The Progeny

Peter's exceptional children

Famous sons

Prominent daughters

Outstanding grandsons

Farther down the family tree

The Proof Is In The Pudding:
Peter's Progeny

In the Loop
If you have a curious mind, you'll be interested in facts that "prove" what has been written about Peter The Great, his children, his grandchildren, and so on down the line. But first, just to pique your interest, we'll tell you here that in 1998, Muscles Yankee (descended from Peter on both his sire's and his dam's sides) won the Hambletonian—a race named after Peter's great-grandsire—with a time of 1:52.2, taking home a purse of $1 million. The following year, a grandson of Peter The Great was selected by a poll of three horse racing magazines as the greatest trotter of the twentieth century. Now, we don't want to stirrup any bad habits here, but—would you care to wager a guess as to which horse the top two trotting world-record holders in the all ages category as of 2006, *and* the winners of two of the top races in 2005, trace back to? We'll get to that in a bit; but first, we'll present some very impressive details designed to assure that you are "in the know" regarding Peter.

"Thank You Sir—May I Have Another?"
The list of children Peter The Great sired that were Standardbred performers had grown at a "phenomenal pace—averaging a hundred or more new [performers] every two years over a period of ten years [roughly 1913-1923]",[227] wrote Hervey in 1947. Peter's "amazing prolificacy", Hervey went on to say, produced "history-making animals, without precedent and in profusion", adding that Peter "showered out performers literally by the hundreds". Along with Peter The Great's "ability to beget extreme speed, he displayed also the capacity to beget extreme *early* speed" (emphasis by the present author). Hervey continued to praise Peter, saying he contributed "champion yearlings, two-, three-, and four-year olds, great money-winners, [and] aged campaigners of prolonged...capabilities".[228] The progeny of Peter The Great have continued to demonstrate what Hervey long ago labeled as the "one all-important attribute" in horse racing: "speed and the ability to beget and produce it".[229]

A Person Could Go Hoarse Talking About Peter's Progeny
In a *W.M.U. News Magazine* article published in the spring of 1963, forty years after Peter's death, writer Leon W. Miller reported checking the summary of eleven consecutive races at a "recent" (that would be recent to 1963) Grand Circuit race meeting, to see how many of the horses were descended from Peter The Great. Miller found that either the sire or the dam, (often both), of the winners, *and* the second place horses, in *each* race, had been sired by a son or grandson of Peter The Great.[230] Ten years later, in a 1973 *Harness Horse Magazine* article titled *"Peter The Great: The Dominant Trotting Family"*, well-known turf writer Ken McCarr elaborated as follows: "It would take many pages of names of famous horses to describe the impact Peter The Great has had on the history of harness horse racing. The best illustration would be to take any pedigree and...see how far back you have to go to find Peter The Great listed. Then keep checking, as he is probably in that lineage more than once".[231] Peter sired many offspring famous for various records and various reasons. And, after we present details of Peter The Great's legendary records, we'll tell you about some of them.

The *Art* of Breeding

Although Peter The Great was not himself a example of perfect breeding, breeders of racehorses did and do look carefully at bloodlines when choosing a stallion to mate with a mare, concentrating them to breed for speed. (By the way, breeding father to daughter, or mother to son, was never common, and breeding of brother to sister is not done; breeding of nieces and cousins is acceptable.)

~ ~ ~

The following article was contributed by the man, himself a breeder of animals, whose concern for Peter The Great's monument resulted in its restoration. There is an art to the breeding of animals, as can be seen in the gracefully worded article below, written the year before Peter The Great was foaled.

~ ~ ~

~~*Tribute To a Master Breeder*~~ *(1894)*

The sculptor lures from the solid marble Images of grace, beauty, or strength that provoke the plaudits of the world···In calling from stone the creatures of his own conception the figures may be shaped at will···Compared with him who has the power to conceive an ideal animal form and call it into life through a profound knowledge of Nature's intricate and hidden Laws, the greatest sculptor is a mere mechanic. There is no higher form of art than that which deals with the intelligent manipulation of animal life: the modeling of living breathing creatures in accordance with the will and purpose of a guiding mind. It rises in its boundless possibilities to heights that are fairly god like. The world of human endeavor presents no nobler field of action, no realm of thought demanding a higher order of ability."

Alvin H. Sanders

Editor of Breeder Gazette, 1894

And The Survey Says...

Why was Peter The Great so enormously successful as a sire? An article that appeared in *The Horse Review* on December 12 of 1917 addressed that very issue. "To account for this wonderful sire, and to detect the secrets of nature which went to his production has been attempted by only those who care to theorize. The more practical students of breeding acknowledge that they do not know the reason, but they do know the facts, and the facts are what they reckon with." ("Facts" apparently meaning Peter's obvious ability to pass on winning traits.) Following that assessment was one very interesting sentence, which offered what may have been the writer's own theory. "However, the deepest students attribute his greatness to the twin facts that [Peter] was himself a very great trotter, and that since he has in his veins none of the blood of either George Wilkes or Electioneer [two other famous sires], he provided a natural outcross for practically every notable mare of the present period." The writer concluded his words with this prosaic statement, likely referring to Peter The Great's phenomenal success as a sire: "But why attempt to reconstruct a problem, the answer to which we already have?" [232]

Can't Touch This

Contemplating that success, *The Horse Review* article added this: "A few facts about Peter The Great as a sire are worth while recording here, for they are vital statistics which go to prove his dominance and to impress upon this generation of horsemen what a marvel he is as a speed progenitor." The article, written in 1917, gives us a fascinating look at what was said about Peter at the time. "Peter The Great leads all living and dead stallions as the sire of standard performers, having the gigantic total of 334 to his credit, of which 44 are new in 1917. He has for the past four years led all sires annually. He is far and away the leader of all sires of 2:10 performers, having no less than 58 in 2:10 or better, 45 of them being trotters. He is likewise the premier sire of extreme speed, having no less that 14 in the 2:05 list, of which nine are trotters."

Seal of Approval

The Horse Review went on with pride, "Perhaps no greater tribute can be paid Peter The Great than the plain and unvarnished statement that [in 1917] he has nine trotters with records of from 2:05 to 2:02, and that their records average 2:03 and 7/9 [ths.]" Wrapping up their view of the situation, *The Horse Review* stated simply, "To continue to enumerate his score of points as the leader of all sires would be a useless task for his achievements are a familiar tale to every horseman. That he is the master–progenitor of all time is universally conceded. There is scarcely a great trotting stake that has been raced during the past fifteen years but has been won by one or more of his sons or daughters." Ample evidence of that Peter's reputation lies in the Laurel Hall handbill below, which tells horsemen plainly that *"If you want a stake horse"* you should *"get a Peter the Great"*. The flyer also posts the names and times of "Twenty-Six Peter the Greats" that were Grand Circuit money winners in 1917; beneath the list is a phrase pointing out that "no other sire" had more than twelve. "Get a Colt by the Greatest of All Sires for $500" ran the words under the list titled *"A Few Bright Stars"*, (words obviously aimed at horse breeders whose billfolds, with that $500 fee, would be depleted by a sum comparable to nearly $8,500 today). Many breeders were willing to pay handsomely for a chance to book a mare with Peter The Great, the sire of so very many winners on the harness horse racing scene.

Handbill from Laurel Hall in Indianapolis features
"THE TRIBE OF PETER THE GREAT...ON THE GRAND CIRCUIT IN 1917"
(Courtesy, Michigan Harness Horseman's Association)

89

A *"Gold Record"* Holder?

If horse racing were like the music industry, it seems that, with so many winning offspring, Peter The Great should have some gold records to his credit. Peter's extraordinary records certainly show that he was a star performer—even as the years passed, and he grew older. When describing Peter's outstanding prowess as a sire, Hervey had this to say in 1947: "The constitutional vigor which he demonstrated is unequaled in breeding records...and this power he retained to his extreme old age, there being two 2:05 trotters in his last crop of foals, [sired] in 1922 at the age of twenty-seven...In all, [Peter The Great] sired thirty trotters in the 2:05 list...[begetting] one or more...in no less than *fourteen* different seasons"[233] during his 25 consecutive (although his first and last seasons were not full) years of stud service.[234]

Peter "Topped The Charts"

Peter The Great's list of Standardbred performers began with Sadie Mac in 1903, when she won her first official race. According to Hervey's 1947 article, the list reached the 100 mark in 1913, the 200 mark in 1915, and the 300 mark in 1917, the year in which Peter became known as the top sire of Standard performers. In 1919, the list reached the 400 mark; in 1921, the 500 mark; and in 1923, the year of Peter's death, the 600 mark. Hervey says that the last of Peter's children was entered in the tables of performers in 1933, when the roster was "for all time rounded out" with 498 trotters and 163 pacers", bringing the total to the "661 record performers" chronicled on Peter's monument.[235] By the close of 1945, the nearest approach—made by any horse—to the prolific sire's number of record performers was that of Peter's son, Peter Volo, who had 532 to his credit at the time.[236] (You'll hear about Peter The Great's two most famous sons, Peter Volo and Peter Scott, soon.) First, let's take off to see some really *super* records set by eight of Peter's children.

"Faster Than a Speeding Bullet, More Powerful Than..."

A racehorse. The fastest of Peter's thirty colts and fillies in the 2:05 *trotting* list was his daughter Mabel Trask (2:01¾), followed by Peter Volo (2:02), The Great Volo (2:02¼), Ethelinda (2:02¼), Mrs. Yerkes (2:02¼), Peter The Brewer (2:02½) and Margaret Druien (2:03), Hervey tells us.[237] (For comparison, the world's fastest trotting record in 2004 was 1:50.2; as we indicated earlier, winning times have improved over the years.) Looking at pacers, we find that Peter sired twelve horses in the 2:05 *pacing* list.[238] The best pacing record was set by "Miss Harris M" (1:58¼), a big mare owned, coincidentally, by Stoughton Fletcher.[239] (The world's fastest pacing record, as of 2004, was 1:46; fascinating to note that today's world's records—both trotting and pacing—appear to have advanced by nearly identical times of roughly twelve seconds in the years that have elapsed since Peter's fastest trotting and pacing children set their records.) When Peter's final statistics were known, the number of performers he had in the 2:10 category had flown all the way to 138 (81 trotters and 57 pacers); there were only two years, says Hervey, in which Peter failed to sire a 2:10 performer.[240]

"Lifestyles of The Rich and Famous"

Let's go "international" here for a moment (courtesy of Dean Hoffman's 1995 article in *Hoof Beats*) to look at Peter The Great's influence overseas. We'll travel first to Europe, where we find that the male line of Victory Song (the fastest trotting son of Peter's grandson Volomite, through his son Peter Volo) is prominent. From there, we'll jet over to Sweden, where sire lines from Peter The Great have been dominating in trotting since the 1940's. While there, we learn that stallion Mack Lobell, one of the greatest trotters of the twentieth century, continues the Victory Song line in Sweden; in addition, according to a 2003 article, "among the Elite mares in Sweden, sire lines from Peter The Great dominate with 93 mares".[241] Next we're off to Italy, where a son of Victory Song sired the spectacular Sharif di Iesolo; in Italy we also find Varenne (1:53), who is descended from Star's Pride (another grandson of Volomite). Peter The Great's influence is felt as far away as Russia, where another of Victory Song's offspring, Reprise, was the dominant stallion at the end of the twentieth century.[242] Now we'll head back to the States to discover, as promised earlier, just which horses there hold the current world-record times.

"Live From New York...It's The Trotting World Record Holders!"
It doesn't have to be a Saturday Night to introduce to you the top two world-record holding trotters, in the "all ages" category, as of early 2006. According to the Harness Racing Museum & Hall of Fame in Goshen, New York, *both* of them trace back to Peter The Great—on both the maternal and paternal sides—through the famous stallion Star's Pride (and thus through Peter's son Peter Volo, mentioned above, to Peter The Great).[243] The current world-record holder is *Tom Ridge*, with a time of 1:50.2, set in 2004 at the Meadowlands track in New Jersey; a stallion foaled in 2001, Tom Ridge set his record as a three-year old. Just behind him is *Victory Tilly*, with a time of 1:50.4, set in 2002 at the same track; a gelding foaled in 1995, Victory Tilly set his record as a seven-year old. The U. S. Trotting Association's list of world-record holders on a one-mile track displays the top three (or four, as some records are tied) horses in the "all-ages"; the one-, two-, three- and four-year old; and the "aged" categories. There are eighteen horses on that exalted list—and a bit or research shows that *each one of those eighteen horses* traces back to Peter The Great.[244]

The *Winners Take It All* in 2005
The Harness Racing Museum & Hall of Fame again provides information, this time about the winners of two top trotting and pacing races held even more recently, in 2005. The winner of the elite Hambletonian (also held at the Meadowlands in New Jersey, and considered by many to be the premier three-year old trotting race in the world) was "Vivid Photo", a three-year old gelding who is descended—that's right—from Peter The Great, again on both his maternal and paternal sides. Vivid Photo won the race (the vivid photo finish of *that* race must have been doubly exciting) with a time of 1:51.2, taking home the winner's portion of a purse worth $1,275,663 for his owner. The 2005 winner of the Little Brown Jug (a premier pacing race held in Delaware, Ohio) was a three-year old named "P–Forty–Seven". If you're wondering whether this horse is also a 'Peter', you're right on the money, and again, on both his maternal and paternal sides. P–Forty–Seven won that race with a time of 1:48.2, capturing the winner's share of a purse of nearly $700,000.

A *Chip* Off The Old Block
Stepping back about a decade in time to look at the 2004 wins from a different angle, it's a cinch to see how dominant 'the Peters' are in the world of harness racing. At Kentucky's Red Mile Track in October of 1994, four-year old Pine Chip, winner of 23 of 24 lifetime starts, broke the world trotting record with a time of 1:51.[245] Amazingly, Pine Chip's world record would hold fast for another *eight years*. With Victory Tilly's victory in 2002 (he was aptly named), he wrested that record from Pine Chip, crossing the finish line with a new world-record time of 1:50.4.[246] Victory Tilly would hold that world-record for two years before it was broken in 2004 by Tom Ridge, who holds the current world-record time of 1:50.2.

The Horse Is Out of The Barn Now
We've sampled some top records on today's harness horse racing scene, and stepped back a bit to look at Pine Chip; now we'll retreat even further, to the first decade of the twentieth century, to discover how Peter's success as a sire began. Would you like to guess whether his early prowess was passed through his sons—or through his daughters? (Get ready, as the answer may surprise you.) If you chose the females, you're a winner. "During [Peter's] early success as a sire, the impression grew up among breeders that Peter The Great would not found a family of his own [through his male line] because of the apparent superiority of his daughters to his sons", Hervey tells us.[247] Peter's supremacy was "unequivocal", he states, for siring daughters who themselves produced many fast horses for the racing scene.[248] In his early years as a sire, Peter's daughters "decisively outclassed his sons; and for that reason it was argued that it need not be expected that the latter would prove great sires".[249] Peter The Great could transmit his superior characteristics through both his female and male lines—an ability that, Hervey implies, is not common.

91

"Turn The Beat Around"

Things changed as the second decade of the century began. Before long, Peter The Great's sons Peter Volo and Peter Scott and "whole galaxy of others", Hervey avows, appeared on the racing scene, sparking a great deal of interest. The outstanding qualities of these horses quickly became apparent (as had been the case with their sire, Peter The Great), and that spark became a conflagration as a "rush to breed to them began", as Hervey phrases it. In his 1995 article in *Hoof Beats* (the official publication of the U. S. Trotting Association), commemorating the centennial of Peter The Great's birth, Dean A. Hoffman extolled the virtues of Peter's two most celebrated sons, asserting that "these two stallions remain the two greatest sources of trotting speed in the world". The Indiana Standardbred Hall of Fame concurred, stating further that Peter Volo and Peter Scott were the "great trotting continuators" of the bloodline of Peter The Great, the bloodline that "overshadows all others on the horse racing scene".[250] Let's have a look at Peter's sons, starting with the two most famous.

Brothers of Another Mother:
Peter's Sons

Most of the sons (and daughters, too) of Peter The Great were of course from different dams. Peter's two most famous sons were no exception: Peter Volo's dam was Nervolo Belle; Peter Scott's was Jenny Scott. Starting with the two most illustrious, we'll take a fast look at some of the famous sons Peter The Great sired, sons that were a result of Peter's breeding with many of the top mares, the crème de la crème, of the entire nation.

Peter Volo (1911–1936)   *Lifetime best: 2:02*

We'll start with Peter Volo. Although he was two years younger than his famous brother Peter Scott, Peter Volo is perhaps best known today, so we've listed him first. Peter Volo was at Patchen Wilkes Farm in Kentucky throughout his racing career, roughly 1912-1915; his sire, Peter The Great (as we know) was there at the same time. During his four years in racing, Peter Volo truly set the harness racing scene aflame, taking world records in the yearling, two–year old, three–year old and four–year old categories. Peter Volo, in fact, won *every race* he started, from his first official race as a yearling, all the way to a match race (a race pitted against just one horse) as a four–year old—after which he retired to stud, greatly sought after as a sire.[251] Dean A. Hoffman tells us that Peter Volo (a black stallion "of rugged and powerful build" that stood 16 hands high) was well known for siring fine trotting and pacing horses. Peter Volo sired his most famous son, the elegant Volomite, at the age of fifteen: Volomite's influence is still felt in both trotting and pacing pedigrees today. Through Peter Volo came the male lines of Victory Song (1:57.3), his fastest trotting grandson, and that of his great–grandson Star's Pride (1:57.1); both male lines trace through Volomite, and both continue to be prominent in harness racing in the twenty–first century.[252]

Peter Scott (1909–1939)   *Lifetime best: 2:05*

Peter Scott, the elder of the two brothers, was the first horse ever to win over $50,000 in stakes and purses in a *single season*. (Figuring that now, it would be considerably over $900,000.) Peter Scott swept the Grand Circuit Stakes in 1915, losing only one of eighteen starts; he was sold that same year for $30,000.[253] (A selling price that would be more than $550,000 now; it was, without a doubt, a very lucrative year for his owner.) Peter Scott sired three horses with records under 2:00: Scotland (1:59¼), Highland Scott (1:59¼), and Rose Scott (1:59¼), all trotters.[254] Through Peter Scott came the male line of the renowned trotter Speedy Crown (1:57.1), who was the "dominant trotting stallion in North America" in the 1990's.[255]

The Million–Dollar Man (Scratch That) *Horse*

Peter The Great's list of money–winning children was headed by his two most famous sons. Peter Scott (2:05) amassed lifetime race earnings of $56,210 (say $1 million now) before he retired to stud, while Peter Volo (2:02) accumulated lifetime race earnings of $44,536 (call it $800,000 now) before retiring. "The exact total of money and number of races won by [Peter The Great's racing sons and daughters] was never calculated", wrote John Hervey in 1947, but "up to 1919 they had won over $800,000 and that they passed the $1,000,000 mark subsequently is certain...their total [number] of races won must have exceeded three thousand."[256] (Don't let today's *individual* equivalents for his two famous sons' winnings confuse you; calculating the *total* earnings in today's financial setting, Peter The Great's moneymaking children would have earned between *$10 and $12 million* in the years leading up to 1919.) With his sons and daughters winning the equivalents of such fabulous sums, we can surely see why Peter The Great was hailed as the "king of sires", and was spoken of with the awe that reverberated throughout the 1917 article published in *The Horse Review*.

Thirteen "Century" Sires...*And Not Only That...*

No less than thirteen of Peter The Great's sons (and at least one grandson) are in the table of "century sires"; that is, they *each* sired at least one hundred performers. According to Hervey's 1947 article, three of Peter's sons (Peter The Brewer, Azoff, and Chestnut Peter) passed the 200 mark [257] and grandson Volomite (Peter Volo's son) passed the 300 mark.[258] Son Peter Volo had 532 record performers to his credit at the close of 1945, making the closest approach (at that time) to Peter The Great's lifetime total of 661 record performers, as has already been noted. Peter The Great sired an amazing 189 sons who also stood at stud, just as their sire had. It is estimated that the number of Standardbred record performers these 189 sons sired "must approximate, if it does not exceed, 5,000", a record, according to Hervey, which literally "throws those of Hambletonian 10 [and others] 'into the shade'".[259]

Hold On, I'm Coming: **More of Peter's Fast Sons**

Besides famous sons Peter Volo and Peter Scott, Peter The Great also sired the following harness racing headliners, many of whom are likely now forgotten. Ranked in order by their lifetime records, we have: The Great Volo (2:02¼) and pacer Peter Stevens (also at 2:02¼), then Peter The Brewer (2:02½), who passed on his extreme speed: he sired the dam of the first *two-year old* to breach the exclusive two minute circle. Others were McGregor The Great (2:03¼), Peter Mac (2:03½), The Senator (2:03½), Hollywood Bob (2:04¾), and Chestnut Peter (2:05¼). And, not wanting to be accused of playing favorites, we will tell you that in addition to Peter Volo and Peter Scott, several other sons of Peter The Great are known for siring horses in the 2:00 lists (both trotting and pacing): Peter Henley (2:02), Dayster (2:05), Laurel Hall (2:06), Azoff (2:14¼), Widower Peter (2:14¾), and Peter Potempkin (2:15¼).[260]

I'm Gonna Be Like You, Dad...You Know I'm Gonna Be Like You"

No "cat's in the cradle" here, (as in the words of the hit folk song back in 1974), but most of Peter's children, like the child in the song, did come to the world, foaled in the usual way. After that, however, many of them were far from "usual". (And, to slip into the lyrical rather than the literal for a moment, we'll point out that any trophies awarded to them certainly might have been silver—although they were not likely to have been silver *spoons*.) Wrapping up our speedy look at the sons of Peter The Great, and bridging the gap to his daughters, we'll tell you that John Hervey's 1947 article quoted Marque as reporting that lots of the offspring Peter sired were like their dad where boots were concerned. "For the most part", wrote Marque, "they [Peter's trotting children] wore a lot of boots—and needed them—in order to protect themselves".[261] Marque went on to say that many of 'the Peters' in their early training "were double or mixed gaited", (Peter had been mixed gaited, as we know), and "that there were no two of the fast Peters whose gaits resembled each other's".[262] Marque concluded with this sentence about Peter The Great's children: "they were with very few exceptions steady. A strong trotting instinct, with brains attuned to perform at the prescribed gait, is one of the family's traits".[263] Strong instincts and brains to boot. Now let's check out Peter's daughters.

93

"She's So Fine":
Peter's Daughters

Fine the daughters certainly were, sharing in those excellent traits, renowned for passing on their sire's outstanding qualities to the foals they produced. Details about Peter The Great's daughters focused almost exclusively on speed: speed that the broodmares passed on to their offspring, and speed that some of his daughters possessed. We'll take a swift look here at Peter's daughters, recounting the tales of the two fastest, and touching briefly on a few others.

No Brooding Over *These* Broodmares

Peter The Great was enormously influential as a sire of daughters who bore winners galore for the harness racing scene. Although there are no records of how many broodmares Peter sired, there *are* statistics regarding the number of record performers those broodmares in turn produced. Hervey notes in his 1947 article that Peter The Great sired dams that produced 902 performers, of whom "117 are in the 2:05 list and 7 in the 2:00 list".[264] Peter The Great's monument in French Lick proclaims that he sired the *dams* of 971 record performers, while an article in the March 1997 issue of *The Michigan Harness Horseman* declares that, in the final summation, an astounding 1,126 (812 trotters and 314 pacers) record performers were credited to Peter's daughters.[265] Peter The Great's bloodline, renowned for its speed, is abundantly represented in the pedigrees of most great broodmares, both trotting and pacing.

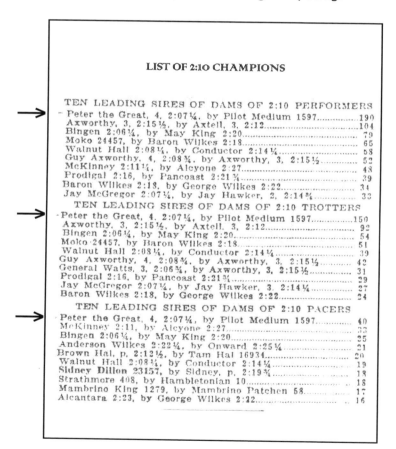

LIST OF 2:10 CHAMPIONS

TEN LEADING SIRES OF DAMS OF 2:10 PERFORMERS

→ Peter the Great, 4, 2:07¼, by Pilot Medium 1597	190
Axworthy, 3, 2:15½, by Axtell, 3, 2:12	104
Bingen 2:06¼, by May King 2:20	79
Moko 24457, by Baron Wilkes 2:18	65
Walnut Hall 2:08¼, by Conductor 2:14¼	58
Guy Axworthy, 4, 2:08¾, by Axworthy, 3, 2:15½	52
McKinney 2:11¼, by Alcyone 2:27	48
Prodigal 2:16, by Pancoast 2:21¾	39
Baron Wilkes 2:18, by George Wilkes 2:22	34
Jay McGregor 2:07¼, by Jay Hawker, 2, 2:14¾	33

TEN LEADING SIRES OF DAMS OF 2:10 TROTTERS

→ Peter the Great, 4, 2:07¼, by Pilot Medium 1597	150
Axworthy, 3, 2:15½, by Axtell, 3, 2:12	92
Bingen 2:06¼, by May King 2:20	54
Moko 24457, by Baron Wilkes 2:18	51
Walnut Hall 2:08¼, by Conductor 2:14¼	39
Guy Axworthy, 4, 2:08¾, by Axworthy, 3, 2:15½	42
General Watts, 3, 2:06¾, by Axworthy, 3, 2:15½	31
Prodigal 2:16, by Pancoast 2:21¾	29
Jay McGregor 2:07¼, by Jay Hawker, 3, 2:14¼	27
Baron Wilkes 2:18, by George Wilkes 2:22	24

TEN LEADING SIRES OF DAMS OF 2:10 PACERS

→ Peter the Great, 4, 2:07¼, by Pilot Medium 1597	40
McKinney 2:11, by Alcyone 2:27	33
Bingen 2:06¼, by May King 2:20	25
Anderson Wilkes 2:22¼, by Onward 2:25¼	21
Brown Hal, p, 2:12½, by Tam Hal 16934	20
Walnut Hall 2:08¼, by Conductor 2:14¼	19
Sidney Dillon 23157, by Sidney, p, 2:19¾	18
Strathmore 408, by Hambletonian 10	18
Mambrino King 1279, by Mambrino Patchen 58	17
Alcantara 2:23, by George Wilkes 2:22	16

Focusing on Peter The Great's daughters, the January 1931 edition of The Horse Review features the Top Ten Leading Sires of Dams whose children rank in these three categories: 2:10 Performers, 2:10 Trotters, and 2:10 Pacers. Peter The Great heads all three lists. (Courtesy, Western Michigan University Archives and Regional History Collection)

Mirror, Mirror, On The Wall: Who Was The *Fastest* of Them All?
No mirror needed, (and no snow or white involved, either). Which's the fairest way to determine the answer? Simply by taking a look at the records, which can be seen quite clearly. The fastest of *all* of Peter The Great's children was a pacer named Miss Harris M: she was the world's first pacing mare to break the two–minute mile.[266] (Miss Harris M, owned by Fletcher, had originally been a trotter,[267] according to *The Horse Review*.) Here's a true tale (although we've given it a story-book opening) describing how fast she was...A long, long time ago, in the not–so–far–away city of Detroit, on July 25 of 1916, four-year old Miss Harris M gave the most sensational performance in the twenty-one year history of the Grand Circuit's $5,000 "B of C" meet. (That purse of $5,000, in the year 1916, would be comparable to a $90,000 purse now.) Miss Harris M took the meet in three straight heats, with grand times of 2:01¼, 2:01¾, and 2:04½.[268] According to a 1916 *Horse Review* article, written just one week after the race, her extraordinary speed in *each* of the three heats had made her "trebly a world's champion": she had beaten the world-record, not once, but *three times,* in one meet.

Once, Twice, Three Times a Lady
Furthermore, in each of those heats, positions on the track had been drawn, not in the customary way, but "by the mercy of the official dice-box", as the 1916 article phrased it. Regardless of the fact that Miss Harris M had won the first heat, the dice (unluckily) gave her the fifth position on the track for the second heat, and then (even more of a handicap), assigned her the *tenth* position in the third heat. In spite of this, Miss Harris M's times were the *fastest three straight heats ever paced by a mare of any age.* Her spectacular performance, in addition to setting the new world's record for four-year old fillies, also made her the fastest performer of any age or sex sired by Peter The Great to that date.[269] (It was an honor she would retain for all time: she would be the only one of Peter's children ever to break the two–minute barrier.) The divine Miss Harris M (1:58¼), the first pacing mare that "ever stepped in even time", received high praise in *The Horse Review* article, which called her "the champion of her sex and gait". (No figure for Miss Harris M's lifetime earnings could be found.)

Mirror Image? Peter's Fastest *Trotting* Daughter
Topping the list of Peter The Great's fastest *trotting* children was Mabel Trask (2:01¾), says Hervey,[270] "a mare of great brilliance and racing capacity".[271] As a five-year old, on July 26 of 1916, Mabel Trask won the $10,000 (that'd compare to over $180,000 now) Grand Circuit "M & M" meet in Detroit in three straight heats, in "splendid form", with times of 2:05¼, 2:07¼, and 2:09¼. Just the day before, Mabel Trask's half-sister had thrilled harness racing fans with her amazing performance at the "B of C" meet in the same city. The back-to-back wins caused a great sensation in the world of harness racing: for the first time in their history, the two top Detroit Grand Circuit classics, one pacing and one trotting, had been won in the same season by children of the same sire—*and each had been won in three straight heats.*[272] Another *Horse Review* article, written in the winter of 1917,[273] proclaimed Mabel Trask "the greatest trotting race mare of all time"; she had lifetime racing earnings of $43,640, (which, for us now, would top $800,000). But could her lifetime trotting record be beaten by her any of her half-sisters later on? Nope. Let's look at their records.

These Females Also Had a Reputation For Being *Fast*
Third on the list of Peter's fast daughters is Margaret Druien (2:03) with earnings of $30,030; fourth is Volga (2:04½), a petite and exquisite light-chestnut champion filly at both the two–and three-year categories,[274] with $25,645. (No dates are known; so no estimates are possible.) Also among his earliest (and fastest) fillies were Grace (2:04¾), and Sadie Mac (2:06¼). Foaled in 1900, it was Sadie Mac whose performances during her unbeaten 1903 season had helped rescue her sire. Sadie Mac would remain undefeated until her sudden death at the age of five, when, sad to say, and to the dismay of racing fans the nation over, she suddenly fell dead during the race that became her final contest.[275] Other notable daughters include Nahma (2:07¼), Czarevna (2:07¼), Miss Stokes (2:08¾), Ethelinda, and Rose Scott, just to name a few.[276] Up next, a peek at two of Peter The Great's most famous grandsons.

Grandsons Are *Awesome*:
Peter The Great's Are Proof of That

Peter's Grandson Greyhound (1932-1965)   *Lifetime best:* (1:55¼)
Now don't go barking up the wrong tree here. Greyhound was not a dog; he was a horse, of course, named for his coat, which was grey in color. Greyhound was a swift racer, just like his namesakes, (which are the fastest breed of dog, able to run at top speeds of up to 45 miles per hour). Greyhound, known early on for slow starts accompanied by superb finishes, was Peter The Great's fastest grandchild: in his racing career, he trotted a total of *twenty-five* two-minute miles.[277] A famous trotting champion whose time of 1:55¼ broke the world's record in 1938, Greyhound would hold that world-record for *over thirty years,* against all attacks, until Nevele Pride (yes, he is also a 'Peter', through Peter Volo) beat him by less than ½ second, claiming the record in 1969.[278] Greyhound, nicknamed "the Grey Ghost", stood 16 hands high; he was a son of Elizabeth, one of Peter The Great's daughters from his last crop of foals (sired at Laurel Hall Farm in 1922, when Peter was twenty-seven years old). Elizabeth's son Greyhound was proof that Peter The Great's power as a great progenitor was still formidable, even late in his life.

Behold...a Pale Horse
Greyhound was the first gelding, as well as the *only* grey, ever to win the Hambletonian, the premier race for three-year olds. Greyhound (whose trainer/driver was the great Sep Palin) was undefeated in his three-year old season, winning 71 out of 82 heats. During his seven years of racing (1934-1940), Greyhound lost only *four* races, three of them as a two-year old; his lifetime earnings were $38,952. (Those earnings, spanning the financially difficult years of the great Depression, would approximate $500,000 in the present economy.) Greyhound, whose grey coat turned pure white after his retirement, *set no less than 25 world records* in his racing career.[279] Ten years after his death, Greyhound was selected as the "horse of the century", (the century being the years 1875-1975), for the one hundred-year anniversary of The Red Mile Track in Lexington, Kentucky. This distinction was commemorated by the placement of a bronze plaque, bearing his name, at the track's finishing line—a finishing line Greyhound had crossed many times when winning a race. In 1999, as the twentieth century drew to a close, polls were taken by three different racing magazines: they chose Greyhound, grandson of Peter The Great, as the

Greyhound's plaque now located at the grandstand. (Photo by Nigel Soult, Red Mile Track Photographer, in 2006)

greatest trotter of the twentieth century—an honor also bestowed upon Peter The Great by the membership of the Harness Horse Association in his home state.

Grandson Volomite (1926-1954)   *Lifetime best:* (2:03¼)
Peter The Great's grandson Volomite (Peter Volo's most famous son) was the first stallion to stand for a $5,000 stud fee.[280] (Depending on what year that fee was set, and translating it into today's equivalents, in the 1930's and early 1940's it could have risen as high as $67,000, while in the post-war years of the late 1940's, it could have fallen as low—*low?*— as $38,000.) Volomite, most famous as a sire of extreme speed in both trotters and pacers, sired 28 horses in the 2:00 category and 198 in the 2:05 category.[281] Two outstanding horses of Volomite's bloodline were Tar Heel (1:57) and Good Time (1:57.4), both exceptional pacing sires.[282] Volomite's lifetime earnings were $32,649,[283] (which today would be something in the vicinity of $350,000). Let's take a look now at some of Peter's more recent famous offspring.

The Far Side (Of Peter The Great's Family Tree, That Is):
Other Famous 'Peters'

We started the story of Peter The Great with a look at some of his illustrious ancestors. And we've read about some of his famous children and grandchildren. Around 1945, half a century after Peter The Great was foaled, horse racing became popular at racetracks near urban areas. World War II was just ending, and change was in the air. The following horses whose roots are intertwined with Peter's were among the tops in the nation.

—Racing in the mid–1940's was *Adios* (1:57½); foaled in 1940, he was a great–grandson of Peter The Great through Peter Volo. Adios (who at one time had belonged to Harry Warner of the Warner Brothers film studio) became a multiple world champion: he set a pacing record that stood for *43 years*.[284]A renowned sire, Adios had lifetime earnings of $33,329. (These were the tight years during and immediately following the war; today's equivalent, roughly $350,000.)

—Also racing in the mid–to–late 1940's was famous sire *Victory Song* (1:57.3); foaled in 1943, he was Volomite's fastest trotting son. Victory Song won nearly $75,000 during his racing career. (Perhaps one–half to three–quarters of a million dollars on today's monetary scene.) Victory Song's male line is very prominent in Europe, and recently in North America as well.[285]

—In 1947, stallion *Star's Pride* (1:57.1), grandson of Volomite, was foaled. Star's Pride was the founder of his own male line; trotters Tom Ridge and Victory Tilly, the world–record holders in the all–ages category in 2006, trace to Peter through Star's Pride, whose lifetime earnings were $140,969.[286] (From today's perspective, those post–wartime earnings would have totaled over $1 million.)

—In September of 1949, at the age of thirteen, Peter's great–grandson *Nibble Hanover* (1:58.4) was sold for $100,000 *cash*, (estimates now would put that figure at over three–quarters of a million dollars cash); the trotter's stud fee was set at $1,000.[287] (Depending on what year that fee was put into effect, Nibble Hanover's stud fees would have roamed from somewhere around $7,500 to $10,000 in present–day money, a considerable fee during that era.)

—In 1953, a list of the "Ten Top Sires of New 2:05 Trotters" had nine—*nine!*—horses that traced directly back to Peter The Great; four of the ten horses had records under 2:00.

—In 1959, pacer *Bye Bye Byrd* (1:56.1) was named Horse of the Year; later, he would become the first to sire a horse also honored with that title. Retired to stud in 1961, Bye Bye Byrd is considered to be the all–time top broodmare sire; in addition, he sired well over 100 horses with 2:00 records.[288] During his racing career, Bye Bye Byrd held twelve world records and had lifetime earnings that soared to over $500,000. (Similar to more than $3 million today.)

—In 1966, pacing champion *Bret Hanover* (1:53 3/5[ths]), great–great grandson of Peter The Great through Peter Volo, was sired by the famous Adios. Bret Hanover won the pacing Triple Crown, as well as being thrice chosen as "U.S. Horse of the Year". In his few years on the racing scene, Bret Hanover amassed winnings of $922,616, (in the vicinity of $5 million now). After his four–year racing season, Bret Hanover was retired to stud, *as yet unproven as a sire*; stud fees were reportedly set at $7,500.[289] (Roughly, that fee would be over $40,000 now.)

—In 1968, *Nevele Pride*, son of Star's Pride, won the Hambletonian with a time of 1:59.2, taking home a purse of $116,190 (a sum over $640,000 in today's money) for his owner. Lifetime earnings of trotter Nevele Pride were $873,238.[290] (Comparable to about $5 million today.)

—In 1968, trotter *Speedy Crown* (1:57.1), founder of his own male line, was foaled. Speedy Crown's progeny have won purses totaling *over $100 million.*[291] Stay tuned for more...

97

Stud Fees and Purses Really Ride The Range

Concluding our tidbits are some impressive details about the high stud fees two of 'the Peters' commanded, as well as some rather startling facts about purses in general. According to an *Indianapolis Star Magazine* article written in 1968, a stallion's stud fee at that time could go all the way up to $15,000, as it had with Adios, son of Peter Volo, and the sire of Star's Pride.[292] (Today, a like fee would add a sleek $80,000 to an owner's pocketbook.) Star's Pride himself, grandson of Peter Volo, was cited as the most expensive *living* stallion at the time the article was written, with a stud fee set at $10,000, (a fee that would bring in something like $55,000 now). The article also provided details about winnings, stating that "a top Standardbred today [1968] can earn anywhere from $100,000 to $1,000,000 in purses". (Shall we do one last calculation, and put that in terms of earning potential in the first half-dozen years of the twenty-first century? It would be similar to a top Standardbred's winnings ranging from $550,000 to a cool *$5 million* in purses.) Stated the *Indianapolis Star Magazine* frankly, "In short, a super sire such as these could make a rich owner a whole lot richer." And with that, we'll close our look at the progeny of Peter The Great, and prepare to bid Peter adieu.

Epilogue

Heads Above The Rest:
Peter The Great

This Has Been No Fairy Tale...

Everything you've read here about Peter The Great's life was drawn from articles written by turf writers who knew horse racing from start to finish. Most of what you've read was written after Peter died, as was the twenty-nine page portion of John Hervey's 1947 book so often quoted here. Of all of the people quoted here who wrote about Peter The Great, Hervey seems to be the only one who actually knew Peter. Hervey's writings, together with the articles written in 1916 and 1917, while Peter The Great was still alive and making his indelible mark on the world of harness horse racing, provided the richness that made Peter come alive for us here.

...And There Was No Fairy Godmother, Either

Nor was there a coach. But there was a sulky, (which is something like it), and there were certainly horses. And there are often mice in barns...

It Wasn't a Glass Slipper, No

There was a sire involved, though. Instead of a girl's slender foot lifted gracefully to slide into a glass slipper, it was a horse's sturdy hoof that was lifted—and the shoe was of iron, nailed on, so that it could not get left behind at the stroke of midnight. The pong of the clock began to sound for eight-year old Peter at the auction, as the minutes ticked away, and no bids were heard. But for chance, the luck of the draw, the fall of the dice, call it what you will, there might not have been a story to tell about Peter. As it turned out, it wasn't a prince who rescued the daughter of a king: it was the daughter of a sire who did the initial rescuing, her success sending Peter to auction, an auction that would place Peter's hoof on the first step of the trail his life would follow. Yet the story ends much the same...

...And So, He Lived Happily Ever After

Peter The Great, king of sires, reigned supreme, the last years of his life filled with sweet green grass, with the many mares with whom he was bred, and crowned with the glory of sharing his life with a good friend. And thus our story ends: the story of a horse from Kalamazoo who helped set the history of harness horse racing, a horse whose spirit lives on in his progeny. We'll let one final quote from *The Horse Review* about the family of Peter The Great bring our tale to its end. "Its members live out races, fight heat after heat...stamina and courage form the family hallmark." *Stamina and courage?* Perfect words to describe Peter The Great.

Back Matter:
The Part That Goes Over The Fence Last

Does what comes last actually matter? Absolutely. As the sun sets on our journey with Peter The Great, and you dismount and hand over the reins, we'd like to offer a parting glance, a summing up, of the major paths in the story of Peter's life. Following the "Afterword", you'll find a brief chronological timeline, (we've made a long story *short* this time), then a recap of Peter's racing record, (presented two ways, first chronologically, then in order of his wins, seconds and thirds). A brief look at Peter The Great's stud career is next, then a quick peek at the famous forebears on Peter's family tree, that peek ending with a more formal pedigree page. (Yes, horses do have them; such records are important, as you know quite well by now.) At the very end, we've tacked on a few bits about harness horse racing in the twenty-first century, for those who've gone the distance and are curious. We'll leave you now to let you explore on your own, and head on back to the barn to see to the horses. What a trip it has been. *Adios!*

~ ~ ~

~ ~ ~

Afterword

To Begin The Beguine...

This book about Peter The Great came together a bit at a time, in a way that was impossible to resist, and I found I simply had to tell Peter's story. In relating how this book came to be, I discovered that the telling of it was so intertwined with the people who contributed to it that many of them are acknowledged personally here. I'll begin where the book did: at the computer.

There's an old saying that you can't tell a book by its cover; I will adapt that here to say that *you can't write a book without a computer.* (However did they write them in the 'BC'—that would be 'before computer'—days? Tons of note cards?)

My first thanks must therefore go to my sister, Nancy Mickenbecker, for her patience and computer expertise. For the many times I have called you or emailed you, early or late, at times convenient and inconvenient, with panicked questions *(what have I done now???)* or with technical questions about how to do this or that, and you always had the answer: Nance, I couldn't have written this book without your help, and I will be forever grateful.

When I couldn't reach Nancy, my alternate computer-help resource was local. I therefore offer thanks of a similar nature to Joel Dryden of Bolt Graphics/The Coffee Cup. To Joel, for his expertise in anything and everything computer or copier; and to both Joel and his assistant, Erin Harris, for their patient and always pleasant answers to my many computer questions, mainly posed by phone, and likely at inconvenient times when they were taking care of customers. (As I don't speak 'computer', their patience has really been amazing). Joel and Erin, I appreciate you both! Thanks must also go to Mary Ellen De Young for her invaluable help with the cover design.

(Having dispensed with the technical aspects of writing the book, I move on now to content: one must have written sources of information from which to write a book, computer or no.)

The Heart of the Book:
The Contents

I began writing a book about the history of Kalamazoo in early January of 2004, not long after my husband and I sold a small business we had owned for over twenty years. (I'm still writing that book; I just got a bit off track when I encountered Peter The Great in my research—telling his story became important to me!) Time passed swiftly. By April of 2005, I'd been working hard on the Kalamazoo book for over a year, and my husband was planning a weekend "guys" trip with some friends. I clearly recall saying to him, a week or so before he was to leave, "I'll just focus on the chapter on Peter The Great while you're gone; there's a finite amount of information about him—I can probably have that chapter done by the time you come home". (*Ha!* That optimistic but erroneous statement could be neatly summed up by two words borrowed from a famous actor in classic western films: *"not hardly"; a*s I write this afterword, the calendar page has just turned to February of 2006!) Here's how this book on Peter The Great, separate from the book on Kalamazoo history, actually got started. I'll thank the major contributors to the book's contents in order of their appearance, as I relate to you the tale of how the "chapter" about Peter The Great became much longer than I'd ever expected—and became a book on its own.

Ellen Taylor
One evening just before my husband's trip, curious about where Peter The Great was buried, (none of the articles I'd read said anything about that), and not content to dismiss the matter without checking, I tried poking around on the Internet to find an answer, and after some time found a site that addressed that issue. The site said that *Peter The Great was buried on the grounds of a hotel in Indiana.* Now, I must admit that struck me as strange. The next day I

phoned the hotel with my question, and was told that there is a monument to Peter, (but not a grave), located on the hotel grounds. I also learned that Peter The Great was an honoree in three horse racing halls of fame. Seeking verification of the honoree information, I decided to call each of the three organizations, and in that fashion ended up talking with Ellen Taylor, Chairman of the Standardbred Hall of Fame in Anderson, Indiana.

I recall our first phone conversation that afternoon last spring. How exciting to discover, not only that Peter The Great had indeed been inducted into that Hall of Fame, but also that Ellen was in her own words a big fan of Peter's, knew a lot about him, and had in fact been party to the movement of Peter's monument from its old location to the new location at the hotel. Ellen and I talked for perhaps an hour, our conversation closing with her offer to send me whatever information she had about Peter The Great.

The packet came by mail a few days later, when my husband was off on his trip. I remember sitting down at the table with it just after supper on that balmy spring evening, the window open and the faint sounds of a lawn mower drifting in on the lilac-scented breeze. Opening the manila envelope, I first looked at the photos she had sent: none of Peter The Great, (I'd known that in advance), but there were some good ones of Peter's monument. Setting the photos aside, I spread the news articles out on the table, choosing to read the shortest ones first. I left a twenty-nine page excerpt from harness racing historian John Hervey's book *The American Trotter* until last, thinking I'd give those pages a quick scan and then read them the next day.

Little did I realize how engrossing that excerpt would be! I found myself caught up in Hervey's account of Peter's story, poring over those pages in the waning light, not wanting to get up even to turn on the lamp: as I finished, the darkness was such that I could barely read the final paragraphs. I owe much of the content of this book to that excerpt by the late John Hervey, whose words are often quoted within these pages. My heartfelt thanks therefore go to Ellen for including Hervey's material, for gathering together that packet of things, and for the hours of time she later spent answering many questions about horse racing (both in conversations and by email). And last, but certainly not least, I thank her for her ever-cheerful attitude and her careful editing of the manuscript: Ellen, it's been a pleasure working with you.

Gail Cunard
Thanks go next to Gail Cunard, Director of The Harness Racing Museum & Hall of Fame in Goshen, New York, for information on current harness racing record-holders, both trotting and pacing. (Gail's organization was one of the three halls of fame I mentioned earlier, and yes, Peter The Great is recognized in their illustrious Hall of Immortals, as you know from the book.) I was thrilled to learn from Gail that Peter's bloodline, which I knew from numerous articles had been very prominent in the first half of the twentieth century, is still very strong today, as evidenced by the details she provided about the current record holders.

Some time after our original conversation, a slim, rolled parcel from Gail arrived out of the blue in our mailbox, containing a wonderful compilation of photos (featured in a supplement to the 1917 Christmas edition of *The Horse Review)* of the estate in Indianapolis where Peter The Great spent the last six years of his life. Not long thereafter, and at separate times, two large envelopes appeared in the mail, also from Gail, containing copies of fascinating 1916 and 1917 articles from *The Horse Review.* I had thought the book on Peter The Great was close to being done when those three extraordinary items arrived last fall; they added more time but oh, they were a wonderful addition to the book, and Gail, I thank you most sincerely for all of them!

Karen Greengard
Next I would like to thank Karen Greengard, member of the Board of Directors of the Michigan Harness Horseman Association, who readily agreed to my request to use her article titled *The Lasting Legacy of Michigan's Peter The Great*, which had appeared in the March 1997 edition of the MHHA magazine. Karen, I enjoyed the quick overview you provided of early harness horse

racing; I thank you for your time, and for telling me during our interesting conversation that, of all of the great sires of Peter The Great's day, Peter's bloodline is the sole line that remains strong even in the 21st century.

Michigan Harness Horseman's Association
Thanks also to Leann Franks of the Michigan Harness Horsemen's Association, first for verifying that Peter The Great certainly had been inducted into the MHHA Hall of Fame, and for afterwards sending me, also out of the blue, the March 1997 magazine that contained Karen's article. Leann, I'm glad you remembered seeing the article, and I thank you for sending it to me.

Indianapolis Star
An article by sportswriter Joe Hamelin in a 1968 issue of the *Indianapolis Star Magazine* had the first and only description I found of how and why Peter's remains were moved from their resting place at the Laurel Hall estate in Indianapolis. The article also had excellent details about some of Peter's famous progeny, and I am thankful for the *Star's* willingness to let me use it.

Dean Hoffman
Also deserving of thanks is Dean Hoffman, turf writer and long-time executive editor of *Hoof Beats* (the official magazine of the U. S. Trotting Association) for giving me permission to use his article *Reflections on The Centennial of Peter The Great's Birth*, which appeared in the May 1995 issue of that magazine. Dean, your article was filled with great information about Peter's life, and it was in your article that I first saw the Xeroxed pictures of Peter The Great that led me to the photos I will talk about next: thanks so much on both counts!

The Soul of the Book:
The Pictures

Ed Keys
Ed Keys, Chief Photographer of the U. S. Trotting Association of Columbus, Ohio, comes next, first for talking with me about photos in Dean's *Hoof Beats* article about Peter The Great, and secondly, for his simple and immediate "yes" to my tentative query as to whether I might be able to use any of those photos for my book. Not only did Ed promptly mail me a CD containing the photos I had seen, but, before it arrived, he surprised me with an email containing a warm and wonderful photograph of Peter The Great and his caretaker/groom Jake Councilman—the first actual photograph of Peter that I had seen! And the CD, when it came, contained ten excellent high-quality photos of Peter The Great, more photos than I had expected. Ed, for that photo permission so quickly granted, for the CD you made and sent, for the patience you exhibited in answering my questions about horse racing—questions like *"what is riding the rail?"* (I didn't speak 'horse' at the time either, and Ellen was out of town for the summer), for the excellent explanation you provided of turn-of-the-century era racing heats: for all of this, I gratefully thank you.

Sharon Carlson
Now, if I were being absolutely accurate, it would be Sharon Carlson, Director of the Western Michigan University Archives and Regional History Collections, who would be deserving of my very *first* thanks for photographs, and articles, about Peter The Great. (The only reason I did not do it that way is that the Archives collections dealt more with Peter's early years in Kalamazoo, whereas these other sources had access to things from a much longer and broader span of Peter's life.) From the beginning of my truly in-depth research on the history of Kalamazoo, Sharon has known exactly where to go and what to look for in the WMU Archives regarding Peter The Great—and anything else I have asked her about. If she didn't happen to have the information available when I first asked, the next day I would find the "you've got mail" flag on the computer, announcing an email from her that invariably contained just what I needed. Sharon, thank you so very much for everything.

103

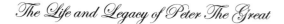

And...The Inspiration

Last, yet most importantly, thanks must go to the late **John Hervey** for the words he wrote about Peter The Great in his book *The American Trotter*, which added incredibly to this story about Peter's life. Hervey wrote for many years for *The Horse Review*, a weekly publication that began in 1885 in Chicago; it provided great coverage of horse racing in general, as well as specifics on horses and horsemen. Hervey, whose articles were said to be "masterpieces", stayed with *The Horse Review* until it's final issue in 1932. John Hervey was 78 years old when *The American Trotter* (still considered to be the "bible" of reference for horsemen) was published in 1947; he died in December of the same year. Hervey's legacy lies in the myriad of articles he penned, in his research of Standardbred bloodlines, in the books he wrote, and in the harness racing awards named in his honor, which recognize excellence in feature writing and video production. Many thanks to The Harness Racing Museum & Hall of Fame for their generous permission to use information about Peter The Great from *The American Trotter*.

Now for these fine folks in Indiana:

Thanks much to two particular gentlemen for speaking with me about Peter The Great: first to Bob Lane, local French Lick historian, (and one of the first people I spoke to in French Lick), for the long and interesting conversations in which he explained to me what he knew of why Peter The Great's monument was on Mount Aire...and also for sending me the *Indianapolis Star Magazine* article about Peter's grave in Indy, and the article about Jake Councilman, (that was given to him by Jake's sister). Many thanks also to Roger Stuckman of Albion, Indiana for sharing his fascinating story about Peter The Great's monument (and other things), and for writing out and sending to me the eloquent *"Tribute To a Master Breeder"*, written in 1894.

I would also like to thank the following people from the area of French Lick, in Orange County, Indiana, for telling me what they in turn knew about Peter The Great and his connection with the French Lick area. To Eva-Sharon Kobee and (again) Bob Lane of the French Lick Springs Resort, and also to Patti Watson and Jim Marshall of the West Baden Springs Dome Hotel and Historic Landmarks Foundation of Indiana, for the warm welcome extended by each of the four while my husband and I were visiting French Lick last summer—and for their invitations to partake in three historic tours of the area. Thanks also to the French Lick Springs Resort for allowing me to adapt their guest map to highlight the previous and current locations of Peter The Great's monument. In addition, thanks to Doug Stevens, manager of the French Lick Springs Resort Stables for information, and to Tom Mills, Diane Dillard, Diana Lopesky, Everett and Norma Davis, and Parke Slick, also of the French Lick area, for chatting with me. And thanks to Jane and Jim Holmes of the American Legion in Indianapolis, Indiana for their research on Peter's monument.

I would like to express special thanks to my family:

To my sister Kathy Wilson, who never fails to ask how the book is going when she calls from Colorado...to my grown daughters, Jen and Kel, for listening to this and that about Peter The Great...and again to Cody who, besides my husband, has been my biggest supporter, one who, despite his eleven years, has asked very sensible questions such as "have you thought about how many pictures you want to use?" or "how many pages do you want the book to be?"

And finally, to my husband Jim:

To Jim, who's hardly had a decent dinner in over two years unless he's made it himself, or we've had company. (In fact, I think he was actually grateful that he had knee surgery recently, for the sheer novelty of having some good meals; I believe he had more home-cooked meals in those two weeks of being home than he did in the two years I have been working on the books!) For his patience, for his sense of humor at the end of the evening, when he is watching the news and I say "just give me a few minutes to wrap things up", (he observed recently that when I say that, it usually takes at least an hour), and for his encouragement when I have needed it most: Jim, our Peter The Great adventure continues still...

Terry Motycka, February 2006

Peter The Great

(2:07¼)

(1895–March 25, 1923)

(The life story of Peter The Great; we'll make a long story short this time...)

Timeline

1895 born at The Oaklands in Kalamazoo, Michigan; breeder: Daniel D. Streeter

1896 yearling at The Oaklands in Kalamazoo, Michigan

1897 raced in the two-year old (Junior) Kentucky Futurity in Lexington, Kentucky; (trainer and driver, Peter V. Johnston) *2ⁿᵈ place*

1898 raced in the three-year old (Senior) Kentucky Futurity in Lexington, Kentucky; (trainer and driver, Peter V. Johnston) *1ˢᵗ place World's record time of 2:12½*

1899 sold to J. Malcolm Forbes for $20,000; placed at stud

February 1, arrived at Forbes Farm in Canton, Massachusetts (near Boston)

August 29, raced as a four-year old in the $10,000 Charter Oak Stake in Hartford, CT; (trainer and driver, Henry Titer) *1ˢᵗ place*

September 4, raced as a four-year old at the Empire City Track in Yonkers, NY; (trainer and driver, Henry Titer) *1ˢᵗ place Set lifetime record of 2:07¼*

September 26, raced as a four-year old in Louisville, KY; (trainer and driver, Henry Titer) *1ˢᵗ place*

October 5, raced as a four-year old at the Transylvania at Lexington, KY; (trainer and driver, Henry Titer) *3ʳᵈ place*

around October 12, raced as a four-year old in the Ashland Stake in Lexington, KY; (trainer and driver, Henry Titer) *2ⁿᵈ place ~Peter The Great's final race~*

stood at stud at Forbes Farm until December 1903

105

Timeline (cont'd)

1903 sold for $5,000 in the Old Glory Auction at Madison Square Garden, NY to Peter Duryea and partner W.E. D. Stokes; to be placed at stud at Patchen Wilkes Farm in Lexington, KY

1904-16 at stud at Patchen Wilkes Farm in Lexington, KY; Stokes sole owner 1906-1916

1916 sold to Stoughton Fletcher III of Indianapolis for $50,000; (possible partner, Thomas Taggart); placed at stud for two seasons at Forkland Farm in Lexington, KY to fulfill previous stud obligations

1918 moved to Fletcher's Laurel Hall Farm and estate in Indianapolis, IN; stood at stud at Laurel Hall Farm for the rest of his life

1923 *Peter The Great died on March 25, 1923 at Laurel Hall Farm, Indianapolis, IN;* head, heart and hooves buried in front of his private bungalow-type barn

1930's Indiana monument to Peter The Great said to have been placed by the American Legion in the mid-1930's, possibly at Laurel Hall Farm, IN

1931 monument to Peter The Great placed at his birthplace, The Oaklands, in Kalamazoo, MI; erected with funds provided by area businessman Charles B. Hays and relatives of Peter The Great's owner, Daniel D. Streeter. Originally placed near the barn where Peter The Great was foaled, the monument was moved to a nearby location sometime after the property was purchased by WMU in 1944. Monument now stands across the street from the Bernhard Center on West Michigan Avenue, west of the Administration Building

1939 ashes of Peter's friend and caretaker, Jake Councilman, spread upon Peter The Great's grave at Laurel Hall Farm in Indianapolis, IN
Please note that this is an approximate, not a confirmed, date.

1962 Peter The Great's remains moved by Warren Atkinson from Laurel Hall Farm in Indianapolis to the former Thomas Taggart estate in French Lick, IN, where they remain today; (grave's location at Laurel Hall Farm in Indianapolis was threatened by street construction). *Please note that this is an approximate, not a confirmed, date.*

1997 Peter's monument moved from former Taggart estate to grounds of West Baden Dome Hotel near French Lick, IN; (move was due to listing of the estate for sale). Hotel currently under ownership of the Historic Landmarks Foundation of Indiana (in 2006); monument has place of honor in a garden setting on hotel grounds

Peter The Great

(2:07¼)

(1895–March 25, 1923)

This list is for those who want to see Peter's races in order by date.

Chronological List of Races

Peter The Great competed in just 7 races in his lifetime

1) As a two-year old in the (Junior) Kentucky Futurity at The Red Mile Track in Lexington, KY; *early October of 1897*. Owner, D. D. Streeter; trainer and driver, Peter V. Johnston. **2ⁿᵈ** *place*

2) As a three-year old in the (Senior) Kentucky Futurity at The Red Mile Track in Lexington, KY on *October 6, 1898*; stakes, $10,000. Winner took $7,300. **Won by 20 lengths**: *set a world record with 2:12½*. Owner, D. D. Streeter; trainer and driver, Peter V. Johnston. **1ˢᵗ** *place*

3) As a four-year old in the Charter Oak Stake at Hartford, CT on *August 29, 1899*; stakes, $10,000. Purse for the winner was $3,225. *"Peter The Great is truly Peter The Great again"*. Owner, J. Malcolm Forbes; trainer and driver, Henry Titer. **1ˢᵗ** *place*

4) As a four-year old at the inaugural meeting of the Empire City Track in Yonkers, NY on *September 4, 1899*; stakes, $5,000. **Lifetime best of 2:07¼** Owner, J. Malcolm Forbes; trainer and driver, Henry Titer. **1ˢᵗ** *place*

5) As a four-year old at Louisville, KY on *September 26, 1899*; stakes, $5,000. Owner, J. Malcolm Forbes; trainer and driver, Henry Titer **1ˢᵗ** *place*

6) As a four-year old in the Transylvania, an all-ages race, at Lexington, KY on *October 5, 1899*. Owner, J. Malcolm Forbes; trainer and driver, Henry Titer. **3ʳᵈ** *place*

7) As a four-year old in the Ashland Stake in Lexington, KY, *around October 12, 1899*; stakes, $3,000. Second week of the "Trots"; Peter The Great was the betting favorite at $225. Owner, J. Malcolm Forbes; trainer and driver, Henry Titer. **2ⁿᵈ** *place*
~Peter The Great's final race~

Peter The Great

(2:07¼)

(1895–March 25, 1923)

*You can't have it both ways? Sure you can. This list is for those
who want to see Peter's racing record by the order in which he won or placed.*

List of Races In Order of Wins, Seconds, & Thirds

Peter The Great competed in just 7 races in his lifetime, statistics as follows:

Wins–4   *Seconds–2*   *Thirds–1*

<u>*Wins*</u>

1) Three–year old (Senior) Kentucky Futurity at The Red Mile Track in Lexington, KY on October 6, 1898; stakes $10,000. Winner took $7,300; ***world record time of 2:12½. Won by 20 lengths***. Owner, Daniel D. Streeter; trainer and driver, Peter V. Johnston.

2) Four–year old Charter Oak Stake at Hartford, CT on August 29, 1899; stakes $10,000. Won $3225; *"Peter The Great is truly Peter The Great again"*.
Owner, J. Malcolm Forbes; trainer and driver, Henry Titer.

3) Four–year old inaugural meeting at the Empire City Track in Yonkers, NY on September 4, 1899; stakes $5,000. ***Lifetime best of 2:07¼.*** *"He can beat any other trotter"* put up against him, it was afterwards said, and *"he can beat the Futurity record if they try with him."* Owner, J. Malcolm Forbes; trainer and driver, Henry Titer

4) Four–year old at Louisville, KY on September 26, 1899; stakes $5,000.
Owner, J. Malcolm Forbes; trainer and driver, Henry Titer.

<u>*Seconds*</u>

1) Two–year old (Junior) Kentucky Futurity at The Red Mile Track in Lexington, KY in early October of 1897. Owner, Daniel D. Streeter; trainer and driver, Peter V. Johnston.

2) Four–year old Ashland Stake at Lexington, KY around October 12, 1899; stakes $3,000. Second week of the "Trots"; Peter The Great was the betting favorite at $225. Owner, J. Malcolm Forbes; trainer and driver, Henry Titer.

<u>*Thirds*</u>

1) As a four–year old in the "all–ages" Transylvania at Lexington, KY, on October 5, 1899. Owner, J. Malcolm Forbes; trainer and driver, Henry Titer.

Stud Career

of

Peter The Great

(2:07¼)

(1895–March 25. 1923)

At the turn of the century, a Standardbred stallion that made creditable racehorses out of 10% of his offspring was considered a success...
~~~
*In his 23 full seasons at stud, Peter The Great became something of a phenomenon, producing early speed, extreme speed, juvenile record-breakers and futurity winners, along with aged campaigners of amazing ruggedness and longevity, with almost miraculous consistency.*
~~~
From his beginning at stud in 1898, through different owners and at different places, Peter The Great had been standing at stud for 25 consecutive years when he died in the spring of 1923.

1898 in Kalamazoo, MI; mated with one mare as a three-year old. Owner, Daniel D. Streeter

1899 at Forbes Farm in Massachusetts; stud service really began this season. Mated with a number of mares; sired 4 foals (one was Sadie Mac). Owner, J. Malcolm Forbes

1900 at Forbes Farm, number of mares or foals produced not stated; sired 5 record performers

1901-2 at Forbes Farm, (stud service restricted while efforts were made to get him back to the races for that season); numbers of mares, or foals produced, is unknown; sired 5 performers

1903 at Forbes Farm; stud career slow to start until Sadie Mac became The Three-Year-Old Champion in the 1903, and had taken the Kentucky Futurity. (Peter The Great's first larger season, as well as his last season in Massachusetts; sired 12 record performers)

1904-15 at Patchen Wilkes Farm in Lexington, KY; twelve seasons at stud. No reliable records available for this time period. *(Peter Scott sired 1909; Peter Volo sired 1911)* Owner, W. Stokes

1916-17 at Forkland Farm in Lexington, KY; two seasons at stud. (Statistics not available.) Owner, Stoughton Fletcher III, for the rest of Peter The Great's life.

1918-1922 at Laurel Hall Farm in Indianapolis, IN for five seasons; last crop of foals in 1922

1923 at Laurel Hall Farm; embarked on sixth season. None of the 6 mares he mated with produced foals. *Peter The Great died March 25, 1923* *(All figures here are taken from p. 410 of John Hervey's book The American Trotter, published in 1947 by Coward McCann, NY.)*

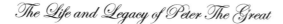

Famous Forebears

on

Peter The Great's Family Tree

(2:07¼)

1895-1923

Famous ancestors who passed along their exceptional characteristics to renowned trotting sire Peter The Great

The Darley Arabian (1700-1730)

The Darley Arabian, a famous Thoroughbred stallion born in Arabia, later became a sire in England. The Darley Arabian was an ancestor some distance back on Peter's family tree.

Messenger (1780-1808)

Messenger, the stallion long considered to be the founding sire of the Standardbred trotter, was born in England, then brought to the United States, where he became a sire. Messenger was Peter's four-times great-grandsire; the relationship is traced through Peter's dam.

Bellfounder (1815-1843)

Bellfounder, a stallion not nearly as well known as Messenger, was also born in England and brought to the United States. Bellfounder was Peter The Great's great-great grandsire; the relationship is traced through Peter's sire.

Jenny Lind (1845-?)

Jenny Lind, a trotting mare depicted winning a race in a Currier & Ives lithograph, was Peter The Great's great-grandam; the relationship is traced through Peter's sire.

Hambletonian 10 (1849-1876)

Hambletonian 10, a stallion that many in the harness racing world today would say has actually come to be best known as the true founding sire of the Standardbred, was Peter The Great's great-grandsire; the relationship is traced through Peter's dam.

Peter The Great's Sire: Pilot Medium (1879-1896)

Pilot Medium, a grandson of Hambletonian 10, was the sire of Peter The Great. Pilot Medium, (the son of Happy Medium, one of Hambletonian 10's four celebrated sons), would later be described as one of the most successful trotting sires of his time.

Peter The Great's Dam: Santos (1887-1916)

Santos, a great-granddaughter of Hambletonian 10 (through her sire), was the dam of Peter The Great. Santos had one unknown ancestor on her maternal side, which sparked doubts about her breeding; those doubts were later disproved.

Peter The Great (1895-March 25, 1923)

Peter The Great, famous trotting sire, is related to Hambletonian 10 on both sides of his family tree. He is the great-grandson of Hambletonian 10 on his paternal side, and a great-great grandson of Hambletonian 10 on his maternal side. Even today, nearly all of the world's champion trotters carry the blood of Peter The Great.

There's a lot more horse history for those who want trot farther down that road: for some fascinating reading, check out the list of sources at the back.

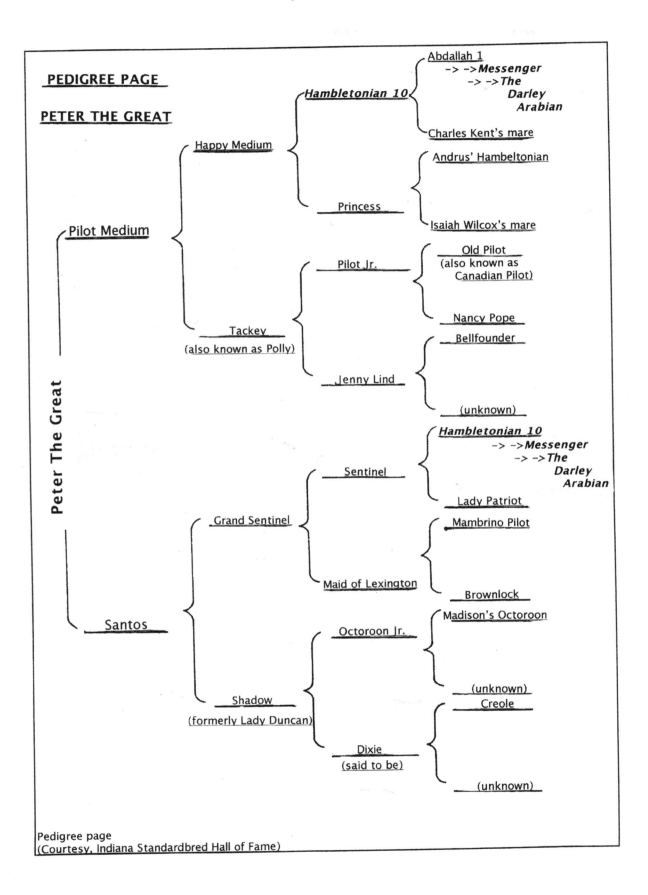

PEDIGREE PAGE

PETER THE GREAT

Peter The Great
- Pilot Medium
  - Happy Medium
    - *Hambletonian 10*
      - Abdallah 1
        -> ->*Messenger*
        -> ->*The Darley Arabian*
      - Charles Kent's mare
    - Princess
      - Andrus' Hambeltonian
      - Isaiah Wilcox's mare
  - Tackey (also known as Polly)
    - Pilot Jr.
      - Old Pilot (also known as Canadian Pilot)
      - Nancy Pope
    - Jenny Lind
      - Bellfounder
      - (unknown)
- Santos
  - Grand Sentinel
    - Sentinel
      - *Hambletonian 10*
        -> ->*Messenger*
        -> ->*The Darley Arabian*
      - Lady Patriot
    - Maid of Lexington
      - Mambrino Pilot
      - Brownlock
  - Shadow (formerly Lady Duncan)
    - Octoroon Jr.
      - Madison's Octoroon
      - (unknown)
    - Dixie (said to be)
      - Creole
      - (unknown)

Pedigree page
(Courtesy, Indiana Standardbred Hall of Fame)

Harness Racing Today:
Trotting and Pacing Combined

Talk About *Mixed Gaits*...
Today the sport of harness racing is governed by the United States Trotting Association, which was formed in 1939. With no further ado, here are a few facts about today's harness racing that can speak for themselves:

On The Track of The Trotting Triple Crown

Today's trotters in the three-year old category compete for their Triple Crown [293], traditionally held at the following racetracks:

—The Hambletonian   held at the Meadowlands in East Rutherford, New Jersey;
                                    purse: guaranteed at $1.5 million total purse

—Kentucky Futurity   held at The Red Mile Harness Track in Lexington, Kentucky;
                                    purse: estimated at $500,000

—The Yonkers Trot   held at the Yonkers Raceway in Yonkers, New York;
                                    purse: estimated at $450,000

In Pursuit of The Pacing Triple Crown

Although Peter's story focuses on the trotting end of harness racing, he sired some exceptional horses for the pacing scene as well. Today's three-year old pacers compete for their own Triple Crown[294], traditionally held at the following racetracks:

—The Cane Pace   held at the Freehold Raceway in Freehold Borough, New Jersey;
                                    purse: estimated at $430,000

—Messenger Stakes   held at The Meadows in Pittsburgh, Pennsylvania;
                                    purse: estimated at $400,000

—Little Brown Jug   held at the County Fairgrounds in Delaware, Ohio;
                                    purse: estimated at $550,000

Something Old, Some Things *"New"*...in Trotting
The *Hambletonian*, first held in 1926, is considered by many to be the premier three-year old trotting race in the world. This Grand Circuit race, which took place for many years in New York, is now held in New Jersey. The *Kentucky Futurity*, which Peter The Great won by twenty lengths in 1898, held its first meet in 1893 at The Red Mile Track in Bluegrass Country in Lexington, Kentucky; the location has never changed. The *Yonkers Trot*, first held in 1899, took place at the Empire City Trotting Club track in Yonkers, New York; it is still held at that track, although the name was changed in 1950 to "Yonkers Raceway".[295] (Wearing of colors by the trainers and horses was first seen at this track, by the way.) The track, with its original grandstand (built of steel, and able to hold 7,500 spectators) cost a total of $780,000, (a turn-of-the-century price tag that would be similar to a whopping $17 million now). The Empire City Trotting Club held its inaugural race on September 4, 1899; festivities on opening day drew a crowd of 12,000 excited spectators who filled the stands to overflowing, all ready to cheer on their favorite horse. Does any of this sound familiar? It should: that inaugural race was won by none other than *Peter The Great*, who in the first heat "took all the wind out of the sails of the pursuit", setting his lifetime record of 2:07¼. Peter, who went on to win the race, felt like the "king of the world", and indeed, it seemed as though his ship had come in. His racing fame would be all too brief...but then, don't some say much of life is a gamble?

Hedge Your Bets?   ~or~   Sometimes You Win; Sometimes You Lose...

Like the gambler in the song, even the most kenny will find themselves doing a bit of both. Many people "hedge their bets" by betting on more than one horse in a race, thus increasing their odds of winning. (The benefit being that one does not risk all on just one horse; rather like the concept to be found in the phrase "don't put all your eggs in one basket".) Betting has accompanied horse racing from its beginning; in the nineteenth century, recognizing an opportunity for increased revenues, various states began legalizing and taxing betting at horse racing tracks.

Wanna Bet?

Today, tracks around the nation use the *pari-mutuel* (a French word meaning "to bet amongst us") system of wagering; invented in France in the 1860's, pari-mutuel bets are not *against the track*, but are *against others who have placed similar bets*. According to the Indiana Standardbred Hall of Fame, odds are based on the relative amounts bet on the horses. Wagering is done on whether a horse will *Win* (this one's obvious), *Place* (finish second), or *Show* (finish third), and each type of bet has its own pool. Some states now also operate facilities for off-track betting (OTB), legalized betting at locations other than the racetrack. This type of off-the-bat betting, (to coin a phrase), in which one merely stops at a nearby facility to place a wager, makes betting more accessible; depending on your position in horse racing, this can be either be a favorable thing—or a handicap. In closing, we point out that we have not attempted to either justify or denounce gambling here, but to simply give the facts, ma'am—just the facts. And we have crossed the finish line now for good.

~~~

~~~

113

Notes

Part One: The Forebears

[1] Karen Greengard, "The Lasting Legacy of Michigan's Peter The Great," <u>The Michigan Harness Horseman</u> May 1997: 35.

[2] "Horse-racing"
<http://www.answers.com/topic/horse-racing>

[3] "The Arabian Horse",
<http://www.ieahc.org/arabian_horse.htm>

[4] The Arabian Horse.

[5] "Historical Standardbreds and Their Foundation Sires-The Darley Arabian".
<http://web.comhem.se/~u52020580/peterthegreatarticle.html>

[6] Historical Standardbreds and Their Foundation Sires-The Darley Arabian.

[7] Horse-racing.

[8] Leon W. Miller, "Horses and Horse-racing in Kalamazoo," <u>Michigan History</u>, Vol. 35, No. 4. Dec. 1951.
<http://www.mi-harness.com/Mich/PeterT.htm>

[9] Miller, Horses and Horse-racing in Kalamazoo.

[10] The Arabian Horse.

[11] "The Standardbred"
<http://www.equiworld.net/UK/horsecare/Breeds/standardbred/>

[12] The Standardbred.

[13] "Historical Standardbreds and Their Foundation Sires-Messenger"
<http://web.comhem.se/~u52020580/peterthegreatarticle.html>

[14] The Standardbred.

[15] Celebrated Horses, Orange County, New York.

[16] "Historical Standardbreds and Their Foundation Sires"
<http://web.comhem.se/~u52020580/peterthegreatarticle.html>

[17] Horse-racing.

[18] "About Harness Racing".
<http://www.georgiandowns.com/about-faqs.htm>

[19] "The Light Harness Vehicle Through the Millennia"
<http://www.rjwalsh.com.au/t-lightharness.html>

[20] The Harness Racing Museum & Hall of Fame in Goshen, New York, verbal information.

[21] "The Inflation Calculator"
>http://www.westegg.com/inflation/>

[22] "The Old Print Shop"
<http://www.oldprintshop.com/cgi-bin/gallery.pl?action=browse&category_id=53,205>

[23] Leon W. Miller, "Peter The Great 2:07¼," W.M.U. News Magazine, Vol. 21, No. 2, Spring 1963.
<http://www.mi-harness.com/Mich/PeterT.htm>

[24] "World of Trotters"
<http://www.worldoftrotters.com/eng-bibl-hambletonian.htm>

[25] Marguerite Henry, Born to Trot (New York: Rand McNally & Company, 1950) 154.

[26] "Hambletonian Milestones 1924 To Present"
<http://www.hambletonian.org/trivia/trtrivia.html>

[27] The Standardbred.

[28] "Historical Standardbreds and Their Foundation Sires-Hambletonian"
<http://web.comhem.se/~u52020580/peterthegreatarticle.html>

[29] Celebrated Horses, Orange County, New York.

[30] The Standardbred.

[31] The Standardbred.

Part Two: The Early Years

[32] "The Roots of Peter The Great," The Michigan Harness Horseman April 1977.
http://www.mi-harness.com/Mich/PeterT.htm

[33] Miller, Horses and Horse-racing in Kalamazoo
and
R. A. Patton, "Made Famous By a Horse," Kalamazoo Gazette 1 Oct. 1944.
http://www.mi-harness.com/Mich/PeterT.htm
and
"Illustrated Atlas of Kalamazoo County,"1890.

[34] Greengard 31.

[35] Patton.

[36] "History of The Oaklands," Western Michigan University, Kalamazoo, Michigan, 2006.

[37] History of The Oaklands.

[38] History of The Oaklands.

[39] Ken McCarr, "Peter the Great–The Dominant Trotting Family," Harness Horse Magazine. 1973: 4–7. <http://www.mi-harness.net/publct/hh/ptrgrt.html>

[40] "1879–1896 Pilot Medium" <http://www.mi-harness.com/Mich/1879.htm>

[41] "Arabian Horse Association—Frequently Asked Questions" <http://www.arabianhorses.org/home/faq/AskExpert4.asp>

[42] John Hervey, The American Trotter (New York: Coward-McCann, Inc, 1947) 394.

[43] Greengard 35.

[44] Greengard 35.

[45] Dean A. Hoffman, "Reflections on the Centennial of Peter The Great's Birth" Hoof Beats: May 1995.

[46] "The Roots of Peter The Great."

[47] Hoffman.

[48] Hervey 419–420.

[49] R. A. Patton.

[50] Hervey 394.

[51] "Johnston Is Part of Turf History," Kalamazoo News Advertiser 2 Feb. 1939.

[52] "The Roots of Peter The Great."

[53] Greengard 35.

[54] Johnston Is Part of Turf History.

[55] The Michigan Harness Horseman.

[56] Hoffman
and
"Johnston Is Part of Turf History"

[57] Hervey 394.

Part Three: The Racing Years

[58] Hoffman.

[59] Hager, Dave, "Peter The Great—A Racing Legend," Kalamazoo Gazette, 1 June 1975.

[60] Miller, Leon W, Peter The Great 2:07¼.

[61] Hervey 394.

[62] Hervey 395.

[63] Patton.

[64] Hervey 395.

[65] Hervey 398–399.

[66] Hervey 395.

[67] "The Roots of Peter The Great."

[68] Hervey 395.

[69] Hoffman.

[70] Hervey 399.

[71] Ed Keys, U.S. Trotting Association.

[72] R. A. Patton.

[73] Hervey 396.

[74] R. A. Patton.

[75] Hervey 396.

[76] Ellen Taylor, Chairman of the Indiana Standardbred Hall of Fame, verbal information.

[77] Hervey 396.

[78] Hervey 397.

[79] Hoffman.

[80] Hervey 398.

[81] Made Famous By a Horse.

[82] Johnston Is Part of Turf History.

[83] Hervey 405.

[84] Greengard 35.

[85] Hervey 398.

[86] R.A. Patton.

[87] "The Oaklands," <u>Western Michigan University</u>, Kalamazoo Public Library scrapbook, Peter The Great.

[88] Hervey 398.

[89] Hervey 398.

[90] Hervey 399.

[91] McCarr, 4–7.

[92] Hervey 398–399.

[93] Hervey 399.

[94] Hervey 399.

[95] Hervey 399.

[96] Hervey 399.

[97] Hervey 399.

[98] Hervey 399.

[99] Hervey 399–400.

[100] Hervey 400.

[101] Hervey 401.

[102] Hervey 401.

[103] Hervey 401.

[104] Hervey 401–402.

[105] Hervey 402.

[106] Hervey 402.

[107] Hervey 402.

[108] Hervey 402–403.

[109] Hervey 403.

[110] Hoffman.

[111] Hervey 402.

[112] Hervey 403.

[113] Hervey 403.

[114] Hoffman.

[115] Hervey 403.

[116] Hervey 404.

[117] Hervey 404.

[118] Greengard 38.

[119] Miller, Peter The Great 2:07¼.

[120] Miller, Peter The Great 2:07¼.

[121] Hervey 404.

[122] Hervey 404.

[123] Hervey 404.

[124] Hervey 404.

[125] Hervey 405.

[126] Hervey 410.

[127] Hervey 405.

[128] Hervey 405–406.

Part Four: The Breeding Years

[129] Hervey 406.

[130] Hervey 420.

[131] Hervey 407.

[132] Hervey 406.

[133] Hervey 407.

[134] Hervey 407.

[135] Hervey 407–408.

[136] Hervey 408.

[137] Hervey 408.

[138] Hervey 408.

[139] Hervey 408.

[140] Hervey 409.

[141] Hervey 420.

[142] Hervey 420.

[143] Hervey 409.

[144] Hervey 420.

[145] Hervey 420.

[146] Hervey 407–408.

[147] Hervey 408.

[148] Hervey 409.

[149] Hervey 409.

[150] McCarr 4–7.

[151] Hervey 411.

[152] Hervey 413.

[153] Greengard 31.

[154] Hoffman.

[155] Mick Heenan, "Bitter-Sweet Acres Belgians", Bloomingdale, Michigan, verbal information.

[156] Hervey 409.

[157] Hoffman

[158] Hoffman.

[159] Hoffman.

[160] Joe Hamelin, "For Some, Greatness is No Accident," Indianapolis Star Magazine 25 Aug. 1968.

[161] Hervey 410–411.

[162] Hervey 409.

163 "Feats of Big Red Trotter Made History," <u>Kalamazoo Gazette</u> 11 Nov. 1948.

164   1)"Historical Standardbred Foundation Sires: Peter The Great".
<<u>http://web.comhem.se/~u52020580/index.html</u>>
  2)"Harness Racing Legend Has Local Ties to Orange County," <u>The News</u> 1 May 1997.
  3) Gayle Cook letter to Margie Hill, hand–written notation states 11 July 1997.
  4) Jeff Bennett letter dated Aug. 26, 1997, to Margie Hill, Chairman of the Indiana Standardbred Hall of Fame.

165 *Author's note:* The gentleman who related this interesting tale heard it first hand; he preferred not to be named, rendering an identifiable footnote impossible.

166 "New Laurels for Peter the Great,"   <u>The Horse Review</u> 2 Aug. 1916.

167 Hervey 410.

168 Hervey 409.

169 Hervey 411.

170 Hervey 413.

171 Hervey 420–421.

172 The Herman Kahn Center of the Hudson Institute" (formerly Laurel Hall); 9.

173 The Herman Kahn Center 9.

174 The New Home of Peter The Great.

175 The Herman Kahn Center 9.

176 Hamelin.

177 Hervey 409.

178 Dave Hager.

179 "The New Home of Peter The Great." <u>The Horse Review</u> Dec. 12, 1917.

180 George M. Gahagan, "Death of 'Jake' Councilman Robs Harness World of Faithful Worker." Unknown paper; date believed to be 8 Feb. 1939.

181 Hervey 411.

182 Hervey 410.

183 Hervey 410.

184 Hervey 412.

[185] "Historical Standardbred Foundation Sires: Peter The Great" <http://web.comhem.se/~u52020580/index.html>

[186] The New Home of Peter The Great.

[187] Hervey 411.

[188] Greengard 38.

[189] Hamelin.

[190] Hervey 411.

[191] Willis F. Dunbar, Kalamazoo and How It Grew (Kalamazoo, Michigan: Western Michigan University, 1959) 141.

[192] Miller, Peter The Great 2:07¼

[193] Hervey 417.

[194] The Herman Kahn Center 9.

[195] Hamelin.

[196] Hervey 409.

[197] Hervey 410.

[198] Hervey 411.

[199] Hervey 409.

[200] Hoffman

Part Five: Peter's Grave & Monuments

[201] The Herman Kahn Center 9.

[202] The Herman Kahn Center 9.

[203] McCarr 4-7.

[204] "History of French Lick and West Baden Springs" <http://www.southernin.com/Pages/archives/may_00/french_lick.html>

[205] Hervey 409.

[206] McCarr 4-7.

[207] "French Lick Springs Resort and Spa" <http://www.travelgolf.com/departments/coursereviews/indiana/french-lick-springs-resort-and-spa.htm>

[208] History of French Lick and West Baden Springs.

[209] French Lick Springs Resort and Spa.

[210] Hervey 409.

[211] McCarr 4–7.

[212] George M. Gahagan.

[213] Hervey 409

[214] The Herman Kahn Center 9.

[215] Hamelin.

[216] Margie Hill, unpublished letters, former Chairman of the Indiana Standardbred Hall of Fame.

Part Six: Honors & Accolades

[217] Greengard 35.

[218] Hoffman.

[219] The Roots of Peter The Great.

[220] Hervey 416.

[221] "Monument Erected to Peter The Great," Kalamazoo Gazette 14 July 1931.

[222] "Monument To Peter The Great," Kalamazoo Gazette 12 Dec. 1940

[223] History of The Oaklands.

[224] Miller, Peter The Great 2:07¼.

[225] Hervey 414.

[226] Greengard 38.

Part Seven: Peter's Progeny

[227] Hervey 411.

[228] Hervey 413.

[229] Hervey 418.

[230] Miller, Peter The Great 2:07¼.

[231] McCarr 4–7.

232 The New Home of Peter The Great.

233 Hervey 413.

234 Hervey 410.

235 Hervey 411–412.

236 Hervey 412.

237 Hervey 415.

238 Hervey 413.

239 The New Home of Peter The Great.

240 Hervey 413.

241 "Important Maternal Lines in Swedish Trotting"
<http://www.worldoftrotters.com/eng-art-svenskeelitston.htm>

242 Hoffman.

243 "U. S. Trotting Association List of World Record Performers"
<http://www.ustrotting.com/misc/world_records/recordperformers.cfm>

244 U. S. Trotting Association List of World Record Performers.

245 "Harness World Records"
<http://www.horseworlddata.com/wrharn.html>

246 "Notes and Names," 19 Feb. 2004.
< http://www.canadiansportsman.ca/articles/nnfeb192004.html>

247 Hervey 416.

248 Hervey 416.

249 Hervey 416.

250 Indiana Standardbred Hall of Fame, verbal information.

251 "Peter Volo," Harness Racing Hall of Fame
<http://www.mi-harness.com/hof/0pq0.html>

252 Hoffman.

253 "Peter Scott," Harness Racing Hall of Fame
<http://www.mi-harness.com/hof/0pq0.html>

254 McCarr 4–7.

[255] Hoffman.

[256] Hervey 414.

[257] Hervey 416.

[258] Hervey 412.

[259] Hervey 416.

[260] McCarr 4–7.

[261] Hervey 414.

[262] Hervey 415.

[263] Hervey 415.

[264] Hervey 416.

[265] Greengard.

[266] "The New Home of Peter The Great.

[267] The New Home of Peter The Great.

[268] "New Laurels for Peter the Great.

[269] New Laurels for Peter the Great.

[270] Hervey 417.

[271] Hervey 417.

[272] New Laurels for Peter the Great.

[273] The New Home of Peter The Great.

[274] The New Home of Peter The Great.

[275] McCarr 4–7.

[276] Hervey 410, 413–416.

[277] "Greyhound (horse)," Wikipedia.
<http://en.wikipedia.org/wiki/Greyhound_%28horse%29>

[278] Hambletonian Milestones 1924 To Present.

[279] Hambletonian Milestones 1924 To Present.

[280] McCarr 4–7.

[281] "Harness Racing Hall of Fame U.S. Inductees"
<http://www.mi-harness.com/hof/index.html>

[282] "Peter the Great: A Standardbred Legend"
<http://www.mi-harness.com/Mich/PeterT.htm>

[283] "Volomite," World of Trotters
<www.worldoftrotters.com>

[284] "Adios," World of Trotters
<www.worldoftrotters.com>

[285] "Victory Song," World of Trotters
<www.worldoftrotters.com>
and Hoffman.

[286] "Star's Pride," World of Trotters
<www.worldoftrotters.com>

[287] Miller, Peter The Great 2:07¼.
   and
   "Nibble Hanover," World of Trotters
   <www.worldoftrotters.com>

[288] "Bye Bye Bird," World of Trotters
<www.worldoftrotters.com>

[289] "Bret Hanover"<www.worldoftrotters.com>
   and Hamelin.

[290] "Nevele Pride," World of Trotters
<www.worldoftrotters.com>

[291] Speedy Crown; "Hambletonian Milestones 1924 to Present"
<http://www.hambletonian.org/trivia/trtrivia3.html>

[292] Hamelin.

[293] "Standardbred"
<http://www.imh.org/imh/bw/standard.html>

[294] "Triple Crown of Harness Racing for Pacers: Encyclopedia."
<http://experts.about.com/e/t/tr/Triple_Crown_of_Harness_Racing_for_Pacers.htm>

[295] "The Yonkers Raceway"
<http://www.yonkersraceway.com/general/history.html>

Sources Consulted

Books

Dunbar, Willis F. Kalamazoo and How It Grew...and Grew. Kalamazoo, MI: School of Graduate Studies, Western Michigan University, 1959.

Henry, Marguerite. Born to Trot, New York: Rand McNally & Company, 1950.

Hervey, John. The American Trotter, New York: Coward–McCann, Inc., 1947.

Periodicals

Greengard, Karen. "The Lasting Legacy of Michigan's Peter The Great." Michigan Harness Horseman May 1997.

Hager, Dave. "Peter The Great—A Racing Legend." Kalamazoo Gazette June 1, 1975.

Harness Racing Legend Has Ties To Orange County." The News May 1, 1997.

"Feats of Big Red Trotter Made History." Kalamazoo Gazette Nov. 11, 1948.

Hamelin, Joe. "For Some, Greatness Is No Accident." Indianapolis Star Magazine Aug. 25, 1968.

Hoffman, Dean A. "Reflections on the Centennial of Peter The Great's Birth." Hoof Beats May 1995.

"Johnston is Part of Turf History." Kalamazoo News Advertiser Feb. 2, 1939.

McCarr, Ken. "Peter The Great-The Dominant Trotting Family." Harness Horse Magazine Dec. 13, 1973.

Miller, Leon W. "Peter The Great 2:07¼." Western Michigan News Magazine Volume 21, No. 2, Spring 1963.

"Monument Erected to Peter The Great." Kalamazoo Gazette July 14, 1931.

"Monument to Peter The Great." Kalamazoo Gazette Dec. 12, 1940.

"The New Home of Peter The Great." The Horse Review Dec. 12, 1917.

"New Laurels for Peter The Great." The Horse Review Aug. 2, 1916.
(Courtesy, The Harness Racing Museum & Hall of Fame in Goshen, New York.)

Patton, R.A. "Made Famous By Horse." Kalamazoo Gazette Oct. 1, 1944.

"The Roots of Peter The Great." Michigan Harness Horseman Apr. 1977.

Unpublished Papers

Hill, Margie. Chairman of the Indiana Standardbred Hall of Fame. Letters to Ellen Taylor, 1997.

Hill, Margie, with Gayle Cook. Chairman of the Indiana Standardbred Hall of Fame. Text for guides at the West Baden Dome Hotel, July 11, 1997.

Hill, Margie. Chairman of the Indiana Standardbred Hall of Fame. Letter from Jeff Bennett, August 26, 1997.

Pamphlets

History of The Oaklands. Handout provided by the Resident Manager of The Oaklands, which is owned by Western Michigan University, Kalamazoo, Michigan.

Lenkowsky, Kate. "The Herman Kahn Center of the Hudson Institute," [formerly Laurel Hall]. Pamphlet, 1991. Hudson Institute, Indianapolis, IN.

"The Oaklands". Western Michigan University. Kalamazoo Public Library Scrapbook on Peter The Great.

Reference Materials

Illustrated Atlas of Kalamazoo County, Michigan. Detroit, Mich.: Wm. C. Sauer; Kalamazoo, Mich.: Ihling Bros. & Everard [distributors], 1890.

Electronic Sources

"About Harness Racing."
18 Mar. 2005 <http://www.georgiandowns.com/about-faqs.htm>.

"The Arabian Horse."
16 Mar. 2005 <http://www.ieahc.org/arabian_horse.htm>.

"Arabian Horse Association—Frequently Asked Questions."
15 Mar. 2005 <http://www.arabianhorse.org/home/faq/AskExpert4.asp>.

"Celebrated Horses, Orange County, New York."
16 Mar. 2005 <http://www.newyorkgenealogy.org/orange/celebratedhorses.htm>.

"French Lick Springs Resort and Spa."
16 May 2005 <http://www.travelgolf.com/departments/coursereviews/indiana/french-lick-springs-resort-and-spa.htm>.

"Greyhound (horse)."
14 Dec. 2005 <http:/en.wikipedia.org/wiki/Greyhound_%28horse%29>.

"Hambletonian Milestones 1924 to Present."
10 May 2005 and 12 Jan. 2006 <http//www.hambletonian.org/trivia/trtrivia.html>.

"Harness Racing Hall of Fame–Peter Scott."
14 Dec. 2005 <http://www.mi–harness.com/hof/OpqO.html>.

"Harness Racing Hall of Fame–Peter Volo."
14 Dec. 2005 <http://www.mi–harness.com/hof/OpqO.html>.

"Harness Racing Hall of Fame U.S. Inductees."
12 Dec. 2005 <http://www.miharness.com/hof/index.html>.

"Harness World Records."
12 Oct. 2005 <http://www.horseworlddata.com/wrharn.html>.

"Historical Standardbreds and Their Foundation Sires."
23 Mar. 2005 <http://web.comhem.se/~52020580/peterthegreatarticle.html>.

"History of French Lick Springs and West Baden Springs."
16 May 2005 <http://www.southernin.com/Pages/archives/may_00/french_lick.html>.

"Horse–racing."
16 Mar. 2005 <http://www.answers.com/topic/horse-racing>.

"Important Maternal Lines in Swedish Trotting."
27 July 2005 <http://www.worldoftrotters.com/eng-art-svenskeelitston.htm>.

"The Inflation Calculator."
Aug. 2005–Jan. 2006 <http://www.westegg.com/inflation/>.

"The Light Harness Vehicle through the Millennia."
18 Mar. 2005 <http://www.rjwalsh.com.au/t-lightharness.html>.

McCarr, Ken. "Peter The Great–The Dominant Trotting Family."
6 Mar. 2005 <http://www.mi-harness.net/publct/hh/ptrgrt.html>.

"The Michigan Harness Horseman."
1 Apr. 2005 <http://www.mi-harness.com/Mich/PeterT.htm>.

The Michigan Harness Horseman, Apr. 1977.
26 Apr. 2005 <http://www.mi-harness.com/Mich/PeterT.htm>.

Miller, Leon W. Michigan History, Vol. 35, No. 4; Dec. 1951.
23 Apr. 2005 <http://www.mi-harness.com/Mich/PeterT.htm>.

Miller, Leon W. Western Michigan News Magazine, Vol. 21, No. 2, Spring 1963.
23 Apr. 2005 <http://www.mi-harness.com/Mich/PeterT.htm>.

"Notes And Names."
12 Oct. 2005 <http://www.canadiansportsman.ca/articles/nnfeb192004.html>.

"The Old Print Shop." 8 Apr. 2005
<http://www.oldprintshop.com/cgibin/gallery.pl?action=browse&category_id=53,205>.

129

"Peter The Great: A Standardbred Legend."
25 Apr. 2005 <hpttp://www.mi-harness.com/Mich/PeterT.htm>.

"Peter The Great: Champion Trotting Horse." 20 Nov. 2005
<http://www.kpl.gov/collections/LocalHistory/AllAbout/recreation/PeterTheGreat.aspx>.

"Standardbred."
20 Mar. 2005 <http://www.imh.org/imh/bw/standard.html>.

"The Standardbred."
24 Mar. 2005
<http://www.equiworld.net/UK/horsecare/Breeds/standardbred/>.

"The United States Trotting Association World Record Performers."
12 Oct. 2005
<http://www.ustrotting.com/misc/world_records/recordperformers.cfm>.

"Triple Crown of Harness Racing for Pacers: Encyclopedia."
2 Jan. 2005
<http://experts.about.com/e/t/tr/Triple_Crown_of_Harness_Racing_for_Pacers.htm>.

Jan. 2006 "World of Trotters."
Mar. 2005 <http://www.worldoftrotters.com/eng-bibl-hambletonian.htm>.

"The Yonkers Raceway."
2 Jan. 2005 <http://www.yonkersraceway.com/general/history.html>.

"1879-1896 Pilot Medium."
12 Oct. 2005 <http://www.mi-harness.com/Mich/1879.htm>.

Other

Gahagan, George M. "Death of 'Jake' Councilman Robs Harness World of Faithful Worker". Unknown paper, date app. February 8, 1939.

Conversations and Emails

Gail Cunard, Director, The Harness Racing Museum & Hall of Fame in Goshen, New York.

Mick and Judy Heenan, owners of Bitter-Sweet Acres Belgians. Bloomingdale, MI.

Ed Keys, Chief Photographer, U. S. Trotting Association.

Ellen Taylor, Chairman, Indiana Standardbred Hall of Fame.

Ronald B. Wiser and Associates Financial Planners of Kalamazoo

Illustration Credits

Front Cover and title page:
This picture of harness racehorse Peter The Great with trainer Peter V. Johnson was caught by a photographer (note the shadows of the spectators as they look on) at the renowned Kentucky Futurity, held at The Red Mile Track in Lexington, Kentucky.
Fall of 1897 or 1898; specific race not identified.
(Courtesy, Western Michigan University Archives and Regional History Collections)

Table of Contents (p. viii)
Peter The Great standing outside the bungalow barn (with flowers gracing the window box) that was constructed especially for him at Laurel Hall Farm in Indianapolis.
Circa 1918–1923.
(Courtesy, U. S. Trotting Association)

Back Matter (p. 99)
The speed of the horses in this image is captured for all time as Peter The Great (with horse Charley Herr coming in behind him) wins the second heat of the Transylvania in Lexington, Kentucky on what appears to be a glorious and windy autumn day.
October 5, 1899.
(Courtesy, U. S. Trotting Association)

The last page of the story (p. 113)
A lingering look at the restored monument (at its new location on the grounds of the nearby West Baden Dome Hotel) provides a fitting end to this story of the life and legacy of famous trotting sire Peter The Great.
Early fall of 1997.
(Photo by Nat Hill. Courtesy, Indiana Standardbred Hall of Fame)

Back Cover:
Vintage photograph of Peter The Great in front of the bungalow home (constructed at Laurel Hall Farm of Indianapolis "especially for the king of trotting sires") offers a window into the richness of the world in which Peter lived during the last six years of his life.
Circa 1918–1923.
(Courtesy, U. S. Trotting Association)

Index

Please note: *In this Index, the name "Peter The Great" has been shortened to "PTG" for simplicity; likewise "Western Michigan University" will be seen as "WMU".*

A

Abbott (& Costello), 66
Abdallah 1, 111. (pedigree)
Adios, 97–98. (*See also* PTG, progeny of)
Administration Building. (*See* WMU)
Allen, Steve, 66
American Legion, 66, 106
American Revolution, 7
American Trotter, The, 19
American trotting history, 7, 75
ancestors. (*See* forebears)
Andrus' Hambletonian, 111 (pedigree)
Apollo, 57
Arabia, 6, 7
Arabian, the Darley. (*See* Darley Arabian)
Arabian, the Godolphin, 7
Arabian head, 19
Arbor Day Drive, 18
Arcadia Brook Golf Course, 80
Art of Breeding, The, 88
artificial insemination, 50–51, 58
ashes. (*See* Jake Councilman, ashes of)
Ashland Stake, (KY), PTG race at, 40, 41, 105, 107, 108
Astor, Henry, 8
Astor, John Jacob, 8
Atkinson, Warren, 68, 106
Austin, Benjamin M., 17
Austin Hersey Dairy Farm, 17
Axtell Track, 10
Axworthy. (*See* Hall of The Immortals)

B

"B of C" (Board of Commerce) meet, 95
Babcock, Robert S., 17
Battle Creek, 20, 75
bay (color of coat), 21
beam of light, (explanation of), 28
Bedouins, 6
Bellfounder, 9, 110, 111 (pedigree)
Benger, Thomas, 8
Bernhard Center. (*See* WMU)
betting, 38–40, 113
    gambling, 113
    illegal gambling,(pre–Depression), 66
    legal gambling, 112–113
    off–track betting (OTB), 113
    pari–mutuel, 113
    wagering, 113
Big Bull, Rysdyk's, 10

Bigelow Hall. (*See* WMU)
Black Beauty (book), 11
Black Hawk, 10
bit, (definition of), 37
blind bridle, (definition of), 37
bloodlines, 6, 8–10, 19–20, 110–111. (*See also* forebears)
Bluegrass Country, 112
boots, (definition of equine equipment), 36
Bret Hanover, 97
British consul in Arabia, 7
broodmares, explanation of, 16
Browne, Samuel A. (Sam), 15–17, 20, 23
Browne Stock Farm, 15, 23
Browne track, 18, 28, 31
Brownlock, 111 (pedigree)
bungalow, (PTG's), 55, 59, 66, 106
Burr Oak Track, 10
Bye Bye Byrd, 97
Byerly Turk, 7

C

California, 64
Canadian Pilot. (*See also* "Old Pilot"), 111 (pedigree)
Cane Pace, The, (Triple Crown, pacing), 112
Capone, Al, 66
castrated, (definition of), 7
Cathedral High School, 68
century sires, 93
Charles Kent's mare, 111 (pedigree)
Charley Herr, (horse), 37–38
Charter Oak Stake, (CT), PTG race at, 37, 105, 107, 108
Chicago, 17, 23, 66
Circus Maximus, (Rome), 6
Civil War, 20
Clark, Walter, 19
Claypool Hotel, (Indianapolis, IN), 51
colt, description of, 16
Cook, Bill, 70
Cook, Gayle, 70
Cook Group, of Indiana, 71
Costello (& Abbott), 66
Councilman, Jake, 56–57, 59, 67, 71, 76, 106
    death of, 67
    ashes of, 57, 59, 63, 67–68, 106
County fair grounds, (in Kalamazoo, MI), 15
Creole, 111 (pedigree)
Crosby, Bing, 66
cutter (sleigh), 42

D

dam, (definition of), 8
Dan Patch. (*See* Hall of The Immortals)
Darley Arabian, the, 6–8, 100, 111 (pedigree)
Delaware, County Fairgrounds, (Triple
    Crown, pacing), 112
Democrat, 64
Democratic National Committee, Chairman of,
    64, 66
Depression, The, 66, 71
Detroit Grand Circuit races
    "B of C" meet, 95
    "M & M" meet, 95
Dixie, ("said to be"), 111 (pedigree)
Driving Hall of Fame, 23
Du Ponts, The, 66
Duryea, Peter, 47–50, 76, 106

E

Egypt, 6
Eighth Wonder of the World, 71
Electioneer, 88
Elite mares, (Sweden), 90
Ellsworth Hall. (*See* WMU)
Empire City Track, PTG race at, 37, 80, 105,
    107–108, 112. (*See also* Yonkers
    Raceway)
Empire City Trotting Club, 112
England, 7, 8, 9
Ethelinda. (*See* PTG, daughters of)
Europe, 97

F

family tree, 6–10, 97–98, 110, 111 (pedigree)
filly, (definition of), 16
Fletcher, Stoughton III, 50–54, 58–59, 63–64,
    76, 90, 95, 106, 109
    bankruptcy of, 64
    banks of, 52
    "tall tales" of, 57
    wife of, 64
foal, (definition of), 9
foal facts, 23
Forbes, J. Malcolm, 34–36, 38, 40, 42–43, 47–
    49, 58, 105, 107–109
    Forbes, "take this horse away", 42–43
Forbes Farm, 34, 47, 49, 75, 105, 109
forebears. (*See* PTG, forebears)
foretop, (definition of), 21
Forkland Farm, 52
founding sires, 8, 7, 8, 10, 110
Freehold Raceway, (Triple Crown, pacing), 112
French Lick Hotel, 64–66
French Lick, (IN), 63–66, 68–70, 106
    map of, 69
    Pluto water of, 64
French Lick Springs Resort, 69
futurities, 28

Futurity. (*See* Kentucky Futurity)

G

Gahagan, Will, 67
gait,
    mixed, 27
    pacer's 27
    trotters, 27
gambling. (*See* betting)
Gateway Golf Course, 80
Gazette. (*See* Kalamazoo Gazette)
gelding, (definition of), 16
George Wilkes, 88
gestation period, (definition of), 16
"gift horse", 48
"going under the wire", (definition of), 7
Godolphin Arabian, 7
Goldsmith Maid. (*See* Hall of The Immortals)
Goshen, (NY), 21, 77–79, 91
Graine, Jud, 23
Grand Circuit, 15, 29, 35–36, 41, 43, 58,
    89, 92, 95, 112
Grand Sentinel, 111 (pedigree)
grave. (*See* Peter The Great, grave of)
Great Volo, The. (*See* PTG, sons of)
Greece, 6
Greyhound, 96. (*See also* PTG, grandsons of)
    "Horse of the Century" for The Red Mile
      Track, [years 1875–1975], 96
    lifetime earnings of, 96
    nickname of, (Grey Ghost), 96
    plaque of, (photo), 96
    world record of, 96
Guy Axworthy. (*See* Hall of The Immortals)

H

Hall of The Immortals, 77–79. (*See also* Harness
    Racing Museum & Hall of Fame, Goshen,
    NY)
Hambletonian, the (trotting race), 87, 91, 96–
    97, 112
Hambletonian 10, (horse), 10–11, 19–21, 51, 57,
    76, 93, 110, 111 (pedigree)
hands, (measurement, definition of), 7
Happy Medium, 10, 19, 110, 111 (pedigree)
Harness Horse Magazine, 36, 49, 64, 66, 87.
    (*See also* Michigan Harness Horsemen's
    Association)
Harness Racing Museum & Hall of Fame, (Goshen,
    NY), 21, 53–54, 77–79, 91
harness racing, (explanations of),
    beam of light, 28
    betting, 38, 66, 112–113 (*See also*
      gambling, pari-mutuel, *and*
      wagering)
    competitive racing times today, 8, 29
    heats, (explanation of), 30
    history of, 6, 10, 75, 98
    horse shoes, (weighting), 27–28, 30, 36

harness racing, (explanations of), *continued*
  how races begin, 28
  "lengths", measurement by, 31
  motorized vehicle, 28
  moving start, 28
  positions, assignment of, 29
  "purses", (explanation of), 7
  "riding the rail", (explanation of), 29
  starting gate, 24
  stud cart, 51
  "wardrobe", (equine equipment), 36, 37
  winning a race, 28
Hartford, (CT), 37, 105, 107–108
Hayes Drive, (Kalamazoo, MI), 80
Hays, Charles B., 80, 106
Hays Park, (Kalamazoo, MI), 15
Headstrong One, the, 7. (*See* Darley Arabian)
heats, (explanation of), 30
Henry Hall. (*See* WMU)
Hervey, John, 19, 21–22, 28–29, 31–32, 34–43,
  47–52, 57–59, 66–68, 77, 83, 87,
  90–95, 98, 109
Hill, Margie, 70
Hill, Nat, (photographs), 70
Historic Landmarks Foundation of Indiana, 70–71,
  106
hocks, (explanation of), 21, 47
Hoekje Hall. (*See* WMU)
Hoffman, Dean A., 34, 41–42, 50, 59, 76–77,
  90, 92
Hoof Beats, (USTA's publication), 34, 41, 50,
  59, 76, 90, 92
"Horse of the Century",
  Greyhound, (for The Red Mile Track), 96
  Peter The Great, (selected by MHHA), 76
Horse Review, The, 34, 51, 53–56, 58–59,
  77, 88–89, 93–95, 98
horse shoes, (weighting of), 27–28, 30, 36, 41
Houston Astrodome, 71
Hudson Institute, 68

I

illegal gambling. (*See* betting)
Immortals, Hall of The, 77–79. (*See also* Harness
  Racing Museum & Hall of Fame, Goshen,
  NY)
inaugural meeting, (Empire City Track, NY) 37,
  80, 105, 107–108, 112
Indiana Standardbred Hall of Fame, 29, 31, 65,
  67, 70, 77, 88, 92, 113
Indianapolis, 50–52, 54, 64, 66–69, 89, 106,
  109
Indianapolis Speedway, 52
Indianapolis Star Magazine, 54, 58–59, 68, 98
insemination, artificial, 50–51, 58
Isaiah Wilcox's mare, 111 (pedigree)
Italy, influence in, 90
  Sharif di Iesolo, 90
  Varenne, 90

J

Jackson, Mrs. Fannie, 80. (*See also* Streeter,
  Fannie)
Janie T., (horse), 29
Jefferson, Thomas, 60
Jenny Lind, (horse), 9, 110, 111 (pedigree)
Jenny Scott, 92. (*See also* Peter Scott, dam of)
Jesuits, 71
jockey, 6
Joe Patchen. (*See* Hall of The Immortals)
Johnston, Peter V., 21, 23, 27–29, 30–32, 34,
  36, 41, 55, 75, 81–82, 105,
  107–108
  gait, PTG, 27
  home on Westnedge Avenue, 23
  horse-shoeing, weighting of, 27–28, 30,
    36
  retirement to lighter duties, 34
  training methods of, 27, 31, 36, 41
  "twenty years ahead of his time", 27

K

Kalamazoo, (MI), 5–7, 9–11, 15–21, 23, 30, 34–
  36, 38, 43, 47, 58, 63, 66, 71,
  75, 80–82, 98, 105–106, 109
  became a city, 16
  racetracks, 10, 15
  The Oaklands. (*See* Oaklands, The)
Kalamazoo County, 15
Kalamazoo Gazette, 17–19, 23, 27–28, 31, 35,
  50, 55, 80–81, 83
Keller, Helen, 66
Kentucky, 38–39, 48–49, 50–51, 54, 64, 91–92,
  96, 113
Kentucky Futurity, PTG races at, 23, 27–29, 30–
  31, 33–35, 43, 75, 81, 105,
  107, 109, 112
  Junior, 27–30, 105, 107–108
  Senior, 30—35, 41, 82, 105, 107–108,
    112
  Streeter's Futurity cane, 33
king of sires, 93, 98
King's Plate, (race), 8

L

Lady Bess, (Civil War horse), 20
Lady Duncan, 15, 111 (pedigree). (*See also*
  Shadow)
Lady Patriot, 111 (pedigree)
Ladywood (school), 68
Laurel Hall, 52–53, 55–56, 58–59, 64, 66–68, 89
Laurel Hall Farm, 50–59, 63–64, 66–69, 76, 89,
  96, 106, 109
Lawson, Thomas W., "betting operator", 38, 40
"lengths", (measurement by), 31
Lexington, (KY), 28–29, 31, 34, 38, 40–42, 48–
  49, 52, 106, 109, 112
lifespan, (horse, explanation of), 16
Lincoln, Abraham, 60
Little Brown Jug, (Triple Crown, pacing), 112

Logan, Will, Jr., 49
Long Island, (NY), 9
Louis, Joe, 66
Louisville, KY, (PTG race at), 37, 38, 105, 107–108

M

MHHA. (*See* Michigan Harness Horseman's Assn)
"M & M" (Merchants' and Manufacturers') meet, 95
Mabel Trask, 90, 95. (*See also* PTG, daughter of)
Mack Lobell. (*See* PTG, progeny of)
Madison Square Garden, 47–48, 106. (*See also* "Old Glory Auction")
Madison's Octoroon, 111 (pedigree)
Maid of Lexington, 111 (pedigree)
Mambrino Pilot, 111 (pedigree)
mare, (definition of), 16
Margaret Druien. (*See* PTG, daughters of)
Markey, Joseph I., 59. (*See also* "Marque")
"Marque", 83, 93. (*See also* Markey, Joseph I.)
Marshall, (MI), 23
Massachusetts, 34, 36, 109
Massachusetts Stake, 36, 105, 107–108
McCarr, Ken, 36, 49, 64, 87, 106
McCracken Hall. (*See* WMU)
McGregor, The Great. (*See* PTG, sons of)
Meadowlands, (NJ), (Triple Crown, trotting), 91, 112
Meadows, The, (PA), (Triple Crown, pacing), 112
'Mecca' (of America), 66, 81
Messenger, 7–8, 10, 110, 111 (pedigree)
Messenger Stake, (Triple Crown, pacing), 112
Michigan Avenue, (Kalamazoo, MI), 80
Michigan, cities in,
    Battle Creek, 20, 75
    Kalamazoo. (*See* Kalamazoo, MI)
    Marshall, 23
    Pentwater, 15
Michigan Harness Horseman, 19, 76, 94
Michigan Harness Horsemen's Association, 76, 89
Michigan Harness Racing Hall of Fame, 77
Miller, James W. (*See* WMU presidents)
Miller, Leon W., 42, 58, 83, 87
Miss Harris M, 90, 95. (*See also* PTG, daughter of)
    world record of, 95
monuments.(*See* Peter The Great, monuments of)
Mount Aire, (IN), 63, 65, 67–70
moving start, 28
Mrs. Yerkes. (*See* PTG, daughter of)
Muscles Yankee. (*See* PTG, progeny of)

N

Nancy Pope (horse), 111 (pedigree)
National Association of Trotting Horse Breeders, 8
National Driving Park, (Kalamazoo, MI), 15
National Hall of Fame of the Trotter, 77–79. (*See also* Harness Racing Museum & Hall of Fame)
National Historic Landmark, 71
neglect, 47–48, 50, 52, 75
Nervolo Belle, 92. (*See also* Peter Volo, dam of)
Nevele Pride, 91, 96–97. (*See* PTG, progeny of)
New England, 35, 75
New Jersey, 91, 112
New York, 8–10, 20–21, 37–38, 47, 75, 77–80, 91, 112
Nibble Hanover, 97. (*See* PTG, progeny of)
North America, dominance in, 92

O

Oaklands, The, 17–20, 23, 30, 34–35, 43, 71, 75, 80–83, 105–106, 109
    after the Junior Futurity, 30
    after the Senior Kentucky Futurity, 34–35
    barn, 18, 20, 23, 35, 43, 75, 80, 82–83, 106
    description of, 17
    elevator, 18
    estate, 80–82,
    horse farm, 17–19, 23, 43, 71, 75, 80–81, 83, 105–106, 109
    log cabin playhouse, 19, 83
    return after Futurity win, 34, 82
    tenant and servant's house, 83
Octoroon Jr., 111 (pedigree)
off-track betting. (*See* betting)
Old Glory Auction, 20, 47, 50, 75–76, 106. (*See also* Madison Square Garden)
Old Pilot, 111 (pedigree). (*See also* Canadian Pilot)
Olympic games, 6
Orange County, (NY), 9, 10
owners, Peter The Great,
    (*See* Duryea, Peter)
    (*See* Fletcher, Stoughton III)
    (*See* Forbes, J. Malcolm)
    (*See* Stokes, W. E. D.)
    (*See* Streeter, Daniel Denison)

P

pacer, description of, 27
pari-mutuel system. (*See* betting)
Patchen Wilkes Farm, 48–50, 52, 76, 92, 106, 109
Patton, R.A., 17–18, 31, 35
pedigree page, Peter The Great, 111
Pennsylvania, (PA), 19
Pentwater, (MI), 15
percentages (of purse) in racing, 7
Peter Scott, 90, 92, 93, 109. (*See also* PTG, sons of)
    bloodlines of, 92
    dam of, (Jenny Scott), 92
    lifetime earnings of, 93
    racing career of, 92

Peter Volo, 49, 90–93, 96–98, 109
    bloodlines of, 92
    dam of, (Nervolo Belle), 92
    lifetime earnings of, 93
    racing career of, 92
Peter The Great
    artificial insemination. (*See* insemination, artificial)
    as a colt, 6, 21, 23, 27–42, 56–57, 71, 76
    as a foal, 22–23, 35, 38, 74–75, 80, 97, 106
    at Laurel Hall Farm, 59, 68, 106
    auction of, 43, 47–49, 76
    birth of. (*See* foaling of)
    bloodlines of. (*See* forebears *and* pedigree page)
    breeding "on shares", 49
    broodmares, (PTG, daughters of), 49, 53, 56, 58, 94
    bungalow home of, 55–56, 59, 67, 106
    buried at, 59, 63, 66–69, 106
        French Lick, 59, 63, 67–69, 106
        Laurel Hall Fm, 59, 63, 66–68, 106
        grave, relocation of, 68–69
    centennial of, 34, 42, 69, 76, 92
    century sires,
        Peter The Great, 93
        children of PTG, 93
    children of, 66, 87, 90, 93–95, 97
        estimate of total earnings of, 93
        similarities to PTG, 93
    color of coat, (bay), 21
    "crème de la crème" of the nation, 58
    cutter (sleigh), 42
    dam of, (Santos), 15, 17, 19–21, 110, 111 (pedigree)
    daughters of,
        Czarevna (95), Elizabeth (96), Ethelinda (95), Grace (95), Mabel Trask (90, 95), Margaret Druien (95), Miss Harris M (90, 95), Miss Stokes (95), Mrs. Yerkes (95), Nahma (95), Sadie Mac (43, 47, 95), Volga (49, 95)
    death of, 59, 106, 109
    description of, 21–22
    early success of,
        daughters, 91, 93–95
        sons, 91, 93
    "false" Peters, 50
    foaling of, 21
    forebears, 6, 8–10, 19–20, 110, 111
        Bellfounder, 9, 110, 111
        Darley Arabian, the, 6–8, 110, 111
        Hambletonian 10; 10–11, 19–21, 51, 57, 76, 110, 111
        Jenny Lind, 9, 110, 111

Peter The Great, forebears, *(continued)*
        Messenger, 7, 8, 110, 111
        Pilot Medium, 9, 19, 110–111
        Santos, 19, 20, 110–111
    gait of, 27, 41–42, 93
    grandsons of,
        Greyhound, 91, 96
        Volomite, 90, 92–93, 96–97
    grave of, 59, 63, 66–69, 106
        at French Lick, 68–69, 106
        at Laurel Hall Farm, 59, 63, 66–68, 106
        location, map of, 69
    grave, relocation of, 68–69, 79
    Halls of Fame, honoree in, 77. (*See also* Indiana Standardbred Hall of Fame, Michigan Harness Racing Hall of Fame, *and* National Hall of Fame of the Trotter)
    head, heart & hooves, 68, 106
    hocks of, 21–22, 47, 51, 59
    "Horse of the Century", 76
    in Kalamazoo, 21, 23–28, 30, 34–35
    "in reverent awe" (at stall of), 35
    influence on, 87–95
        daughters, 91, 94–95
        sons, 91–93
    insemination, artificial, 50–51, 58
    international influence in, 90
        Italy, 90
        Russia, 90
        Sweden, 90
    "king of sires", 66, 98
    "king of the world", 38, 112
    leading sire of, 94, 97
        2:10 pacers, 94
        2:10 trotters, 94
        dams of 2:10 performers, 94
        new 2:05 trotters, 97
    lifetime best record, (2:07¼), 37, 71, 81, 105, 107–110
    lifetime earnings of, 42
    "mantra" of, 75
    monuments of, 6, 63, 66–71, 80–81, 90, 94, 106
        French Lick, (IN), 6, 63, 65, 66–71, 77, 90, 94
            former location of, 63–69
            inscription on, 71
            Laurel Hall, (possibility of), 66–67
            map of, 69
        Kalamazoo, (MI), 6, 80–82, 106
            inscription on, 81
            location of, 80
        West Baden, (IN),
            current location of, 69–71
    neglect of, 47–48, 50, 52, 75
    owners of. (*See* each name for additional information)

P *(continued)*

Peter The Great, owners of, *(continued)*
    Duryea, Peter, 47–50
    Fletcher, Stoughton III, 50–59
    Forbes, J. Malcolm, 34–48
    Stokes, W.E.D., 48–50
    Streeter, Daniel Denison, 15–20, 23–35
  pedigree page of, 111
  'Peter went to sleep', 59
  progenitor, as a, 71, 76–77, 88–89, 96
  progeny of, 83, 87–98
    Adios (97–98), Bret Hanover (97), Good Time (96), Highland Scott (92), Mack Lobell (94), McElwyn (92), Muscles Yankee (87), Nevele Pride (91, 97), Nibble Hanover (97), P–Forty–Seven (91), Peter Scott (90, 92), Peter Volo (90, 92), Pine Chip (91), Reprise (90), Rose Scott (92), Scotland (92), Sharif il Iesolo (90), Speedy Crown (92, 97), Star's Pride (90, 92, 97–98), Tar Heel (96), Titan Hanover (97), Tom Ridge (91), Varenne (90), Victory Song (90, 92, 97), Victory Tilly (91, 97), Vivid Photo (91), Volomite (90, 92–93, 96–97)
  purchase price, (paid by),
    Duryea and Stokes, 47–48
    Fletcher, 50–51
    Forbes, 34
  racing career, 29–42, 107–108. (*See also* races)
    chronological list of, 107
    list by wins, 2nds and 3rds, 108
  racing career of, detailed,
    Ashland Stake, (KY), 40–41, 107–108
    at Louisville, (KY), 38
    Charter Oak Stake, (CT), 37, 105, 107–108
    Empire City, inaugural race, (NY), 37, 96, 99, 105, 107–108, 112
    Junior Kentucky Futurity, (KY), (2-year old), 28–30, 105, 107–8
    Senior Kentucky Futurity, (KY), (3-year old), 30–35, 105, 107–108
    Transylvania, the, (KY), 38–39, 105, 107–108
  "rags to riches", 58
  sire, as a, 5–7, 21, 35, 43, 48–49, 50–51, 55–56, 58, 70–71, 76–98
  sire of, (Pilot Medium), 9, 19–21, 111 (pedigree)
  sleigh (cutter), 42
  sons of, 93 [all names]
    Azoff, Chestnut Peter, Dayster, Hollywood Rob, Laurel Hall, McGregor The Great, Peter Henley, Peter Mac, Peter Potempkin, Peter Scott, Peter Stevens, Peter The Brewer, Peter Volo, The Great Volo, The Senator, Widower Peter
  stallion king, 55, 58
  "stand in reverent awe" (at stall), 35
  Standardbred performers sired, (list compiled by hundred's, and by year attained), 90
  stud career of, 35, 41–42, 48–51, 54, 57–58, 66, 76, 90, 93, 90, 106–107, 109
  stud fees of, 35, 49–50, 58
    $2,500, 35, 58
    "$100 rising to $1,000", 58
  studbook of, 49
  The Oaklands, at, 21, 23, 27–28, 30, 34
  'the one thing', 59
  "thin", 48, 52
  timeline of, (chronological), 105–106

  trainers of. (*See* Johnston, Peter V., *and* Titer, Henry)
    training methods of
      Johnston, 27, 31, 36, 41
      Titer, 36–41
  "versus Hambletonian", records of, 57
  world record of, 31, 105, 107, 108
  yearling, as a, 23, 27
Peter The Great, Russian czar, 23
Philadelphia, (PA), 8
Pilot Jr., 111 (pedigree)
Pilot Medium. (*See also* forebears) 9, 19–21, 111 (pedigree)
Pittsburgh, (PA), 112
Pluto water, 64
Polly, 9, 111 (pedigree). (*See also* Tackey)
Princess, 111 (pedigree)
progenitors, 71, 76, 88
  Hambletonian 10; 10, 76
  Peter The Great, 10, 76
progeny, 83, 87–98
purchase price paid for,
  Hambletonian 10 and dam, 10
  Lady Duncan (Shadow), 15
  Peter The Great, 34, 47–48, 50–51
  Pilot Medium, 19
  Santos, 20
"purses", definition of, 7
  percentages of, 7

Q

"quest for information", 63

R

Race Street, (Kalamazoo, MI), 15
races, Detroit Grand Circuit,
    "B of C" meet, 95
    "M & M" meet, 95
races, Peter The Great's. (*See* PTG, racing career
    of)
races, Triple Crown, pacing, 97, 112
    Cane Pace, the, 112
    Little Brown Jug, the, 112
    Messenger Stake, the, 112
races, Triple Crown, trotting, 112
    Hambletonian, the 96–97, 112
    Kentucky Futurity, the, 112
    Yonkers Trot, the, 112
racetracks. (*See also* races)
    in Kalamazoo, MI
        Axtell Track, 10
        Burr Oak Track, 10
        County fairgrounds, 10
        National Driving Park, 15
        Recreation Park, 15
    other,
        County Fairgrounds, (OH), 112
        Empire City Track, (Yonkers
          Raceway), (NY) 37, 107
        Freehold Raceway, (NJ), 112
        Meadowlands, the, (NJ) 112
        Meadows, (PA), 112
        Red Mile Track, The, (KY) 29,
          91, 96, 107
        Union Course, New Orleans, 10
        Union Course, New York, 9
racing, explanations of. (*See* harness racing,
    explanations of)
racing times, (competitive today), 8
Ras el Fedowi, 7. (*See also* Darley Arabian)
Readsville, (MA), 36
record performers, 57, 71, 77, 87–90,
    93–94, 98, 109. (*See also*
    Standardbred performers)
Recreation Park, (Kalamazoo, MI), 15
Red Mile Track, The. (*See* racetracks, other)
Reprise. (*See* PTG, progeny of)
"riding the rail", explanation of, 29
Roach, Tom, (photographs), 65, 67
Rockefeller, Nelson, 66
Roman nose, description of, 11
Rome, 6
Russia, influence in, 90
Rysdyk, William, 10
"Rysdyk's Big Bull", 10

S

Sadie Mac, 43, 47, 75, 95, 109
St. Peter's, Rome, 71
Sanders, Alvin, 88. (See also *Art of Breeding*)
Sangren, Paul V. (*See* WMU)
Santos, 15, 17, 19–21, 110, 111 (pedigree)
Sentinel, 111 (pedigree)

Shadow 15, 111 (pedigree). (*See
    also* Lady Duncan)
Sharif di Iesolo. (*See* Italy, influence in)
Siedschalg Hall. (*See* WMU)
Single G. (*See* Hall of The Immortals)
sire, definition of, 7
Soult, Nigel, (photograph, Greyhound plaque), 96
Speedy Crown, 92, 97. (*See also* PTG,
        progeny of)
    bloodline of, 92, 97
    purses won by progeny of, 97
Stadium Drive, (Kalamazoo, MI), 17. (*See also*
    Territorial Road)
stallion, description of, 7, 16
"stallion king", 55, 58
Standardbred,
    description of, 10–11
    explanation of, 8
Standardbred performers, 57, 71, 77, 87–90,
    93–94, 98, 109. (*See also*
    record performers)
standing at stud, explanation of, 8
Star Pointer. (*See* Hall of The Immortals)
Star's Pride, 90–92, 97–98. (*See also* PTG,
        progeny of)
    bloodline of, 92
stock market crash, 66
Stokes, W. E. D., 48–51, 58, 106
Strader, Robert S., 52
Streeter, Amelia, (wife of Daniel D.), 17–18
Streeter, Blanche, (daughter of Daniel D.), 18
Streeter, Daniel Denison, 15, 17–21, 23, 27–30,
        33–35, 43, 47, 81–82, 105,
        107–109
    barn of. (*See* Oaklands, The, barn)
    death of, 20, 23
    family of, 17–19, 82
    Futurity cane of, 33
    horse farm of, 17–19, 23, 43, 71, 75,
        80–81, 83, 105–106, 109
    log cabin playhouse of, 19, 83
    sale of PTG to Forbes, 34–35
    The Oaklands, 17–20, 23, 30, 34–35,
        43, 71, 75, 80–83, 105–106,
        109
Streeter, Fannie, (daughter of Daniel D.), 18, 80.
    (*See also* Jackson, Mrs. Fannie)
Streeter, Milford B., (brother of Daniel D.), 80
stud, description of, 8
stud career. (*See* PTG, stud career of)
stud cart, description of, 49
stud fees, explanation of, 8, 50
studbook, entries in, 49
Studebakers, the, 66
sulky, description of, 6, 9, 28
Sweden, influence in, 90

T

Tackey, 9, 111 (pedigree). (*See also* Polly)

Taggart, Thomas, 51, 64–66, 68–69, 106
    estate and mansion of, 64–69, 106
    "possible partner in PTG purchase", 51
    "took over Fletcher's farm", 64
"taking down the purse", 7
teeth, (neglected, explanation of), 48
Ten Top Sires of New 2:05 Trotters, 97
Territorial Road, (Kalamazoo, MI), 17. (*See also* Stadium Drive)
The American Trotter, (book by John Hervey). (*See American Trotter, The*)
The Oaklands. (*See* Oaklands, The)
Thoroughbred, 6, 8
Titan Hanover, 97. (*See* PTG, progeny of)
Titer, Henry, 36–41, 105, 107–108
    training methods of, 36–41
Tom Ridge, (horse), 91, 97
Tommy Britton, (horse), 40
trainers of PTG. (*See* Johnston, Peter V., *and* Titer, Henry)
Transylvania, PTG race at, 38–39, 105, 107–108
Triple Crown. (*See* races, Triple Crown, pacing *and* races, Triple Crown, trotting)
"Trots", the, 31, 38, 40, 107–108. (*See also* Kentucky Futurity)
trotter,
    American, 7, 9
    description of, 27
    training of, 28
trotting pitch, explanation of, 10
Trotting Register, John Wallace's, 8
Turner, Lana, 66

U

USTA. (*See* U.S. Trotting Association)
USTA's *Hoof Beats,* 41, 76, 92
U. S. "Horse of the Year",
    Bret Hanover, 97. (*See* PTG, progeny of)
    Bye Bye Bird, 97. (*See* PTG, progeny of)
U. S. Trotting Association, 30, 39, 52, 55–56, 76, 91–92, 112
uncastrated, definition of, 7
Union Course, New Orleans, 10
Union Course, New York, 9
university. (*See* Western Michigan University)

V

Van Ranst, Cornelius, 8
VandeGiessen Road, (Kalamazoo, MI), 80
Varenne, 90. (*See also* Italy, influence in)
Victory Song, 90, 92, 97.(*See also* PTG, progeny of)
Victory Tilly, 91, 97. (*See also* PTG, progeny of)
Vivid Photo, 91. (*See also* PTG, progeny of)
Volomite, 90, 92–93, 96–97. (*See also* PTG, grandsons of)
    bloodline of, 92, 96
    lifetime earnings of, 96

W

wagering. (*See* betting)
Wallace, John, 8
"wardrobe", (equine equipment for PTG), 36, 37
Warner, Harry, 97
Warner Brother's Film Studio, 97
Washington, George, 60
Washington Square, (Kalamazoo, MI), 15
weanling, definition of, 23
West Baden, (IN), 63, 65, 69–71, 106
West Baden Dome Hotel, 63, 65, 69–71, 106
    garden setting of, 70, 71, 106
West Michigan Avenue, (Kalamazoo, MI), 80, 106
Western Michigan College, (now WMU), 83
Western Michigan University, 17–18, 20, 80–81, 83, 106
    Administration Building, 80, 83, 106
    Bernhard Center, 17, 20, 80, 106
    Bigelow Hall, 20
    Ellsworth Hall, 20
    Henry Hall, 20
    Hoekje Hall, 20
    McCracken Hall, 83
    Miller, James W., *President of*, 83
    Sangren, Paul V., *President of*, 83
    Siedschlag Hall, 83
Western Michigan University Archives and Regional History Collections, 5, 22, 32–33, 75, 77, 94
Western Michigan University News Magazine, 42, 58, 83, 87
Westnedge Avenue, (Kalamazoo, MI), 23
Wilbur Home and School for the Feeble–Minded, 20
Winings, Greeley, 53, 54, 58
withers, definition of, 7
world record holders, "all ages" category, 87, 91
    set in 2002, 87, 91; record still holds in 2006
    set in 2004, 87, 91; record still holds in 2006
World War I, era of, 59, 64
World War II, era of, 97

X

Y

yearling, definition of, 9
Yonkers, (NY), 37, 105, 107–108
Yonkers Raceway, 112. (*See also* Empire City Track)
Yonkers Trot, the, (Triple Crown, trotting), 112

Z

About the Author

Terry Motycka was born and raised in a suburb of Chicago, and met her future husband there. After their marriage they moved to Kalamazoo, Michigan, started a family, and purchased a grocery store in a small nearby town. An avid reader, Terry found herself fascinated by the history of Kalamazoo; often caught relating historical tidbits to her family and friends, she resolved that one day she would turn those tidbits into a book. Some years later, after she and her husband sold their business, Terry began gathering facts in earnest and started laying them out in chapters. One of the surprising facts she encountered was that in 1895 Kalamazoo had been the birthplace of a famous trotting horse.

Intrigued, Terry began to research the sketchy facts that were available, intending to write what she thought would be a short chapter. That chapter grew into a book on its own. *The Life and Legacy of Peter The Great* is Terry's first book, and precedes the book on the history of the city, which she plans to call *Kalamazoo: Things You Never Knew*. Terry and her husband Jim are blessed with two lovely adult daughters and three delightful grandchildren, who combine to not only keep them busy but to make life very special for them. The couple has a home in Portage, Michigan, which they share with their two 'rescued' dogs.

(Photo taken at The Oaklands by Jim Motycka)